Teaching for Realists

Realists

Making the education system work
for you and your pupils

Omar Akbar

BLOOMSBURY EDUCATION
LONDON   OXFORD   NEW YORK   NEW DELHI   SYDNEY

BLOOMSBURY EDUCATION
Bloomsbury Publishing Plc
50 Bedford Square, London, WC1B 3DP, UK
29 Earlsfort Terrace, Dublin 2, Ireland

BLOOMSBURY, BLOOMSBURY EDUCATION and the Diana logo are trademarks
of Bloomsbury Publishing Plc

First published in Great Britain, 2021

A catalogue record for this book is available from the British Library

ISBN: PB: 978-1-4729-8528-6; ePDF: 978-1-4729-8529-3;
ePub: 978-1-4729-8527-9

2 4 6 8 10 9 7 5 3 1

Typeset by Newgen KnowledgeWorks Pvt. Ltd., Chennai, India
Printed and bound in the UK by CPI Group Ltd, Croydon CR0 4YY

To find out more about our authors and books visit www.bloomsbury.com
and sign up for our newsletters

Contents

1 Introduction 1

2 Why teaching is the best job in the world 5

3 How to make the curriculum work 9

4 How to overcome pupil apathy 21

5 How to make paper *work* 31

6 How to manage all things data 43

7 How to survive against the Ofsted odds 55

8 How to manage behaviour policies 69

9 How to use rewards effectively 85

10 How to build positive relationships with your pupils 91

11 How to get the support you need 99

12 How to be a happy teacher 105

Index 108

Chapter 1
Introduction

What this book isn't about

The UK education system is often on the receiving end of much criticism from all stakeholders, namely teachers, parents, pupils and academics. It seems that it is often the case that the politicians who dictate the system and the aforementioned stakeholders do not see eye to eye. Discussing the specifics of these grievances would take up several books, but in any case, the aim of this book is not a call for an overhaul of the system. It is not to sing the praises of the Finnish education system and suggest which parts of it we should adopt. It is not to tell you how ineffective homework is and why it should be abolished. It is not to tell you how out of date the curriculum is and how it should be revitalised. It is not to tell you how unfair exams are and why we should do away with them. It is not about the benefits of smaller class sizes and it is not about the perils of school budget cuts.

While a book analysing the above would be useful to policymakers, such a book would have no effect on the daily practice of teachers – particularly new teachers – who ultimately are bound by the system. In other words, as tempting as it may be to teach whatever you want and not give your class practice paper after practice paper in the lead-up to an exam, you simply don't have a choice. There is, however, a lot you can do to make your life easier *and* help to improve your pupils' experiences of school.

And that's where this book comes in.

What this book is about

Allow me to be absolutely direct: there are some aspects of the education system (or inevitable by-products thereof) that are at best pesky, at worst detrimental but mostly somewhere in between. In this book, you will not only learn about the nature and extent of these problems but, more importantly, you will also learn what you, as a teacher, can do to overcome or manage them effectively.

Take, for example, the curriculum. There are several issues that arise from it that adversely affect pupils, but there are many ways in which you can work around these so that you achieve the maximum benefit but stay within the boundaries of the system. In addition to this, while doing your training you probably learned very quickly that the majority of pupils you teach are nowhere near as motivated as you were when you were at school. Were you taught how to *actually* overcome pupil apathy, or were you just told to 'be positive' and reward the kids who 'do well'? Here you will learn how best to overcome this approach and have a lasting impact on your pupils.

Almost every school uses some form of behaviour policy to manage behaviour. One issue with the system is that no matter how supportive the school, the education system does not allow for a teacher's dependency on behaviour policies, and consequently their overuse is seen as a weakness. This book will teach you the many subtle and not-so-subtle ways in which good, experienced teachers stop misbehaviour dead in its tracks before doing so much as giving a child a warning.

No doubt you will have been told of the importance of building relationships with your pupils to best manage behaviour and enable academic success, but were you ever told how good teachers do this? Unfortunately, there is a disconnect between the importance that the system places on relationship-building and the guidance that the system (and therefore schools) offers on how best to do so. You'll be surprised at how much of this is in your control and the level of impact that you can make by doing the right things.

The education system has an irrational obsession with the monitoring and scrutiny of teachers. At more or less any school you teach, you will find that, in one way or another, you are always jumping through hoops, always being made to prove yourself. While there is little you can do to oppose this significant issue (at least in terms of your daily practice), there is a lot that you can do to better manage things such as observations and book scrutinies in order that you do your best and avoid being caught out. Even something like an Ofsted inspection can be a lot more bearable if you know what you're in for and how to respond.

As well as high levels of bureaucracy, another issue that goes hand in hand with the former is that of accountability. Rightly so, teachers are accountable for their teaching and their pupils' results, but many in the edusphere feel that the levels of accountability placed on teachers are unrealistically high, adversely affecting both pupils and teachers alike. Again, while we have little say over accountability levels as classroom teachers, there is much that we can do to manage them better for ourselves and our pupils.

It is very common for new/trainee teachers to be offered high levels of support in the early years of their career. Unfortunately, the excessive demands of the system do not allow these expectations to be met, and new teachers often find that there is a disconnect between the level of support offered and the level of support available. Here you will learn the true nature of the support offered in schools, as well as how best to access it.

Finally, as it is no secret that teacher wellbeing and happiness are persistent issues in education, you will be given some less obvious guidance on how to be a happy teacher.

Why this book was written

Often, new teachers enter the profession not knowing what to expect in particular areas, and this can lead to frustration and anxiety – which, quite frankly, are avoidable. The sense of disillusionment isn't necessary, and the time wasted on trial and error could be very easily spent elsewhere.

Your teaching, your pupils' outcomes and your overall sense of job satisfaction would be much improved if you simply had a coffee with an experienced teacher and asked them what you can do to make the education system work for you.

Think of this book as exactly that.

But before we begin, let's remind ourselves why we're here.

Chapter 2
Why teaching is the best job in the world

While the focus of this book is on the obstacles in the education system and how best to overcome them, it does not take away from the fact that teaching is indeed the best job in the world. It is worth reminding yourself of this from time to time.

If you were to phone – sorry, text – some of your non-teacher friends (from now on, refer to them as 'civilians') and ask them whether the world is a better place because of what they do, how do you think they'd respond? Truth is that the overwhelming majority will either say no or will not be able to give you a firmly positive answer.

Because of you, however, the world is a better place.

We aren't superheroes (although I'm convinced that we are) but never, ever forget the level of impact that you have. Everything from the clothes you wear to the content you teach and the phrases you use – kids will remember it all. You will be walking through the vegetable (or the alcohol?) aisle of a supermarket and hear someone shout 'Sir!' or 'Miss!' They'll approach you with a big smile and tell you how they're now at university and thank you for getting them there. Kids will visit you five, ten or even 20 years after they've left and tell you how much they miss your lessons and how grateful they are for having had you as a teacher. You'll eagerly await results day and cry tears of joy when your kids open the envelope. You'll be upset when a class you've taught for years finally has to say goodbye, and when you get a two-page thank you note from the quietest kid in your Year 8 class, you will treat it in the same way you would were it a card from your niece.

We actually don't have to think too hard to remember our teachers at school. I can recall a time during a French lesson when my friend scrunched up a piece of paper and threw it at the teacher, near missing her. She blatantly saw what happened but chose to ignore it. He thought that he'd got away with it, but the next day – you will never believe this, and God knows what would happen to a teacher if they did this in 2021 – while we were working in silence, she scrunched up a piece of paper, threw it directly at my friend, hitting him clean in the forehead, and, in her thick French accent, said, 'See? I got you back now.' From my science teacher who got me two As to my philosophy teacher who taught us what it really means to think, I remember them all.

Whether it's for your crazy sense of humour, your astounding ability to explain complex concepts or your capacity to inspire, you will be remembered. While they may not always show it directly, kids know that we are a key variable in determining their future life chances and this is why they hold us so dearly even years after they've left us. Civilians will never truly understand the feeling of being remembered, whereas much of a child's future life success will in some way be attributed to us. What a privileged position to be in!

Yes, civilians have it easier and they don't have to deal with half the amount of shit that we do, but they don't have anywhere near as much fun either. While they're trapped at their desks all day, you get to watch your kids throw water balloons at the deputy head during the school fayre and you get to partake in staff-versus-students football matches. You get to use your humour and personality to relate to people, and when kids don't stop talking, you get to stand up, make your serious face and say corny stuff like, 'Err, it's your time you're wasting.' You get to banter: when you ask your class, 'Any questions?', you get to laugh when one of them replies, 'Sir, can I go to the toilet?' You get to smile when you're super-anxious about an Ofsted inspector coming into your room and a kid says, 'Oh my God, Sir. Stop brickin' it. You're a good teacher.' I vividly remember one time when a kid was wearing a bright yellow jacket in the building and I asked her to remove it because it was 'blinding me'. Her response? 'When the light reflects off your bald head it blinds me too, but you don't hear me complaining!' Sometimes you just have to laugh along.

Every teacher has their aura. Whether we know it or not, we are constantly teaching kids how to navigate their way through life as well as academia. Psychologists tell us that we become the people we spend time with, so it follows that some of what a teacher is will ultimately form part of what a pupil will become. Yes, teaching is a career that involves some degree of acting, but rarely does a teacher leave their deeply held values at home. I can recall complaining to my history teacher, 'Why do we have to know history? It's already happened! What can you even be with history anyway?' He replied, 'Is that what everything's about in life? What you want to be?' He could have just told me to shut up and get on with it but he chose to give me a deeper message. You get to give a deeper, lasting message that civilians will never understand the feeling of. One of my deeply held values is that the minds of young people will survive and thrive if they're encouraged to be independent in their thinking and discouraged from being swayed by the crowd, the advertising companies, the politicians, the celebrities, the… [insert as appropriate]. Above my whiteboard in big letters, it says: 'What's right is not always popular; what's popular is not always right.' What special message will you give your pupils?

As you read these pages, know that identifying problems and dealing with them is not contrary to your love of teaching. In fact, it is perfectly normal to both love and hate teaching at the same time. What will determine your belief that yours is the best job in the world, however, is how much of your mind's attention you decide to focus on the aspects that you love, while, at the same time, properly managing the aspects that you don't.

You *can* make the education system work for you and your pupils.

Good teachers do it every day.

Chapter 3
How to make the curriculum work

No doubt at some point before you decided to become a teacher, you thought about your previous teachers – the way they taught, the less obvious skills that you picked up from them, the lively discussions that took place in their lessons. You no doubt compared the way in which they taught to the way that your future self wanted to teach and imagined yourself becoming an amalgamation of them all.

The good thing is that you still have the freedom not only to get a bit crazy in the classroom, but also to contribute to the holistic development of the children just like your favourite teachers did, which is probably why you still hold them in such high esteem.

There is, however, one potentially pesky obstacle: the curriculum. But fear not – if you're clever about it, your lessons can be as engaging as some of the ones that you remember from your school days, and your pupils will thank you in decades to come for teaching them a lot more than just the prescribed content/skills. While there is a degree of wriggle room, and the way in which middle and senior leaders choose to organise and interpret the National Curriculum varies, many in education cite a number of problems with what can be generically dubbed 'the curriculum'.

The problems with the curriculum

Too narrow

One of the biggest complaints from teachers – and pupils probably think the same but don't know any better – is that the curriculum is too narrow in two areas: knowledge and skills. While the problem is the same in all key stages, it manifests itself differently in primary and secondary schools.

In secondary schools, changes to school accountability measures that have taken place within the last few years have meant that arts subjects carry less weight than English, maths, science, humanities and languages when measuring a school's success. What this has meant is that particular pupils who want to do art or music, for example, could very easily be denied this choice and instead be forced to do a subject that 'counts'.

Meanwhile in primary schools the heavy focus on English and maths in Year 6 due to the SATs exams has led to a very narrow curriculum in Year 6 in many schools. In essence, the more pressure on the school to achieve high SATs results, the less diverse the curriculum. Even science (which 'counts' in secondary schools) is often reduced to the absolute minimum, to the point that pupils who leave primary schools with satisfactory grades in English and maths still enter secondary school not knowing that the planets revolve around the sun.

The above obviously refers to the curriculum in the broader sense, i.e. which subjects are being taught, so a classroom teacher does not have much influence in this matter. However, many teachers considered the curriculum to be too narrow long before any of the changes in recent years. The reason for this is that even *within* a given subject, we are often prescribed, very specifically, exactly what to teach. This, in and of itself, is not the worst thing ever – it makes sense for all the kids in the country to be taught the same thing. The problem, however, is that while much of it is essential foundation knowledge, some of it was very blatantly decided arbitrarily by some bureaucrat at some conference somewhere, with little or no consultation with anyone who has ever taught a lesson in their life. And you have to teach it all, with almost no flexibility. Frustrating for both teachers and pupils alike.

Inaccessible

At the same time that the curriculum became narrower, it also became less accessible than it has ever been – at least in my lifetime. The then education secretary, Michael Gove, decided that the previous curriculum was too easy (it wasn't!) and in one fell swoop made changes that essentially meant that parts of A level content crept their way into GCSE, and primary school pupils were learning concepts such as fractions as early as age five. As well as teachers having to take on the borderline-impossible task of simplifying concepts, teachers noticed a sense of apathy – or, rather, a sense of defeat – from many pupils, who seemingly disengaged from learning altogether. It seems that the new curriculum is responsible for a degree of demoralisation of pupils and teachers alike.

Lack of skills

As it stands and has always stood, the curriculum by and large focuses on the development of a child's cognitive skills – for example, sustained attention, selective attention, divided attention, long-term memory, working memory, logic and reasoning, auditory processing and visual processing. Of course, this is not without merit: cognitive skills are not only essential for any career but they are also essential for one's daily functioning as a human being. The curriculum should indeed focus on the development of cognitive skills – it really is a no-brainer (pun intended).

There is, however, an under-focus on non-cognitive skills such as conscientiousness, perseverance, teamwork, character, problem-solving, social skills, work ethic, community responsibility, organisational skills, communication skills, resilience, self-management and creativity, which schools usually encourage as an 'add-on' or develop implicitly rather than explicitly.

Not so ironically, employers often complain that young people, while being very well qualified on paper, often lack 'work skills', particularly self-management, resilience, perseverance, commitment and a sense of urgency. By no means is school the only factor involved in the development of these skills (a child's home environment has a greater impact), but the imbalance of focus means that the education system is not doing everything in its power to develop pupils sufficiently in order for them to reach their full potential in the workplace. Ironically, non-cognitive skills are also key predictors of academic success.

So surely, common sense would dictate that the imbalance be redressed? One cannot help but think that the reason why it hasn't is due to the fact that non-cognitive skills are difficult for schools to measure. I can't imagine an exam board awarding Joe Bloggs 70 per cent in his resilience and perseverance exam. If schools can't measure them, the government can't measure schools. If the government can't measure schools, then they can't show off how much they've 'improved' schools. Call me cynical.

This can be disheartening for teachers like myself who want nothing more than to believe that we are preparing our kids for the 'real world' and want to play a key role in their holistic development. You see, it's not just employment that non-cognitive skills are essential for. Research has also shown that the degree of non-cognitive skills possessed by a child is a significant predictor of positive outcomes in adulthood overall, including in less obvious areas such as relationships and mental health.

How to make the curriculum work

Make it easy

If you've been teaching for any length of time, you will know that the only way to teach a difficult concept is by breaking it down into small chunks and informally assessing along the way. One would think, then, that the problem of inaccessibility could be solved by simply utilising your teaching expertise. Unfortunately, while good teaching can overcome some of the issue, the problem goes much deeper.

When we teach, we often assume that our pupils possess a degree of prior knowledge, and in any case, we normally recap prior knowledge before teaching anything new. Due to the nature of the current curriculum, it is advisable to make an adjustment to the way in which we do this. Firstly, whatever you are teaching, you are better off assuming that pupils have no prior knowledge *whatsoever*, i.e. recap everything from Year 3 if you're teaching in Year 6 and from Year 7 if you're teaching in Year 11, rather than doing what most of us do, which is just to recap the work from the previous stage. The reason for this is because there is a good chance that: a) they haven't seen the topic before; b) they've seen it before but didn't spend the necessary time on it, so the knowledge isn't embedded; or c) they found it too difficult the first time and so didn't fully engage with it. And of course, it goes without saying that they could've just forgotten!

Many a new teacher will get given a topic rota and eagerly dive in, only to find themselves screaming, 'They know absolutely fuck all!!!'

a week later. You can make the curriculum more accessible and save yourself a lot of headaches if you teach a given topic as if you are teaching it *from scratch*. Rest assured, the knowledge will most probably be in there somewhere – you just have to spend a bit of time getting it out of them. 'Who's got time for that?!' I hear you ask. Granted, time is a potential factor but *quickly* repeating the basics will save you time in the long run.

'Bin the curriculum'

This was what my NQT mentor told me once upon a time when I struggled to teach a class who were off the walls – literally. As kids – younger or older – are more focused on the here and now than they are on the future, you will struggle to get many pupils to engage with fractional distillation by simply telling them that it will help them get a good GCSE or increase their employment prospects.

Of course, my mentor did not actually want me to 'bin the curriculum' (surely, I'd have got binned too if I'd done that?). What he meant was go *outside* the curriculum, i.e. make the curriculum relevant to real life and/ or the daily lives of pupils. Let it be known from the outset that you will not be able to do this every lesson, every topic, but injecting it wherever possible will do wonders for your teaching and 'jazz up' potentially dry areas of the curriculum. Here's an example:

The components of air (mostly nitrogen and oxygen) can be separated using a process known as fractional distillation. As a science teacher, I've taught this to pupils who are inherently interested in science – for any number of reasons – and to pupils who aren't so much, again for any number of reasons. For *both*, I make a point of showing them a video of some poor kid getting a giant wart frozen off by a doctor using liquid nitrogen. I play it at the start of the lesson without saying a single word, and watch while the pupils scream, 'Eeeeeee Sir! That's disgusting! What you showing us this for?!' Once it's over, I question-probe, eventually asking them where nitrogen comes from in the first place.

The freezing of warts using liquid nitrogen is not on the syllabus. The reason why I choose to incorporate it is because, as well as engaging the pupils, it makes the lesson more memorable and the topic more relevant to real life. Try to make 'binning the curriculum' part of your lesson-planning repertoire, as engaging with the 'irrelevant' will make pupils more likely to engage with the 'relevant'.

Before you do, a quick health warning: 'binning the curriculum' does not – and must not – equate to mindless entertainment. Relying on the latter to engage your pupils sets you up for failure, primarily because you won't be able to keep it up and the moment that you're not entertaining, you'll be faced with a bunch of moody kids telling you how shit your lesson is. If, however, pupils' entertainment is *incidental* to 'binning the curriculum', then by all means embrace it. Otherwise, choose *interesting* over entertaining when planning your lesson. One other thing: keep an eye on the time – you still have a curriculum to get through, so don't spend the whole lesson telling kids about your warts. Five minutes every few lessons – or wherever possible – is sufficient.

Tell a story

On that note, another way to enrich the curriculum is by telling a story or anecdote relevant to the topic that you're teaching. You may go slightly off topic as above, but don't feel obliged to make it funny, have some big punchline or otherwise be entertaining. Again, if it is, so be it, but what makes for an effective story is not the level of emotional response that you can generate in pupils. Rather, the best stories are the ones that are personal to you. Unfortunately, 'prim and proper' teachers leave the story-telling to the teachers who are 'cool' or 'down with the kids', perhaps because they assume that for stories to be effective, both the teacher and the story have to be daring. This is not true. As corny as it sounds, your pupils are interested in you, no matter who you are. (If you don't believe me, randomly show up with glasses or contact lenses one day and watch how many questions you get!) So, if you've got something that you can tell them about plant nutrients without telling them about the time when you decorated your university halls of residence with the road signs you stole on the way home from a nightclub, then go for it!

In order to make story-/anecdote-telling also part of your lesson-planning repertoire, all you have to do is ask yourself, 'Can I relate this to me?' If you can, inject a story into your lessons every so often. Accept, however, that it can't always be done and there is no need to overreach, i.e. if you don't have an interesting story involving plant nutrients then don't go telling the kids about the time you got stung by a cactus when you were in Egypt – they literally have nothing to do with each other. When I'm teaching about the relationship between force, mass and acceleration, for example, I tell the kids about my boxing days and how difficult it was to spar with bigger guys. When I'm teaching about DNA, I show them the results of an ancestry test I once took and link it to how stupid racism really is, given the fact that pretty much everyone is mixed race to a certain extent. When I'm teaching about the different stages of drug manufacture, I tell them about the time at uni when we tested a drug on a guinea pig's intestines. It had to be killed before the intestines could be extracted, and this meant that the professor had to hold it by its body, raise it up to arm's length and then bash its head against the desk before a mid-line incision could be made (don't judge me – that was the official procedure!). You get the idea.

When telling a story or anecdote, again, be particularly mindful of the time. Kids will have lots of questions about your stories (or even accuse you of animal cruelty, as they did me), and as tempting as it can be to go with the flow, they still have to make progress in the lesson, not just find out more about you! Perhaps save the stories for near the end of the lesson. Also, while it is by no means essential to have a story, feel free to make one up. I mean, you're going to have to tell a few lies to your line managers at some point in your career ('I swear I entered my data – it must not have saved!' 'My Year 8 books were in my car, which got stolen. I marked them, honestly!'), so you might as well practise on the kids.

Developing non-cognitive skills

The extent to which non-cognitive skills can be taught is very much debated. Can you actually teach a child how to be conscientious? Probably not, but non-cognitive skills can definitely be nurtured. As the education system has not ignored non-cognitive skills entirely, schools normally do this in two ways. Firstly, non-curriculum time, i.e. tutor time, assemblies or days off timetable, can be used to encourage these skills by explaining their relevance to the workplace, etc. Secondly, teachers may teach their lessons in such a way that requires pupils to use – and therefore develop – non-cognitive skills. Currently, the latter does not feature as much in the curriculum as it perhaps should. Nonetheless, it's something that all teachers can incorporate into their everyday practice while still making sure that they cover the curriculum they're required to teach, and so it will be the focus of this section.

For anyone who isn't aware, did you know that if you connect a fruit in a circuit it will act as a battery and produce a voltage? Seriously. In science, pupils have to know the scientific method, which is more or less a standard that can be applied to any experiment. As well as getting pupils to do the fruit battery experiment and explaining scientific method in that context, I use the opportunity to simultaneously develop their non-cognitive skills.

Pupils are divided into groups and each is given a different scenario. For example:

'You are a group of international scientists who have just discovered a new fruit called "fruitataria". You have found out that this fruit can act as a battery that is 100 times more powerful than an orange. You are going to do a presentation to show your audience how you discovered this.'

All pupils are given the same guidance:

- You may not read from a book.
- Everyone in the group must speak.
- It must be exciting and engaging.
- It must be two to three minutes long.
- You must mention independent, dependent and control variables.
- You must describe how you ensured accuracy, reliability and validity.
- If you don't like the scenario, you can make up your own! But you must include everything above.

In short, pupils work together to design and present a role-play on the experiment that they've just completed, using the guidance above. How many non-cognitive skills can we identify in this activity?

- Collaboration: They're working in groups. If I decide not to allow friendship-based groups, I'll make a point of telling pupils that when they're adults they will have to work with people irrespective of whether or not they like them.

- Creativity: The activity encourages pupils to think outside the box by taking on a specific role. (If pupils stereotype scientists by acting 'geeky', I will use it as an opportunity to dispel myths.)

- Social skills: If I don't let them work with their friends, pupils will be forced to speak to those with whom they are less comfortable.

- Perseverance: This is a hard task to do well. Many pupils will want spoon-feeding but will not get it!

- Communication: Knowledge has to be conveyed in a way that their audience understands. This will encourage pupils to be mindful of the importance of succinctness, which is particularly important in scientific communication.

- Self-management: They can't get away with doing nothing. With tasks like this, pupils will try to avoid being on the spot by putting most of the responsibility for speaking onto an agreeable pupil. Some will moan about having to speak, at which point I tell them that this type of task is common at interviews for professional jobs – in other words, employers will want people with presentation skills. If you don't start to develop them now, when will you?

Another lesson that nurtured non-cognitive skills – created by primary school teacher and prominent children's book blogger Emily Weston (tweets @primaryteachew) – is outlined below:

The theme of the lesson was 'inference', i.e. reaching a conclusion on the basis of evidence and reasoning. Pupils were divided into groups of five and each was given a different shoe (or a picture of one). One group, for example, may have been given a pair of high heels, another a football boot, etc. The shoes also had a worn appearance. Upon viewing the shoe, pupils were required to make inferences about the character of its potential wearer. The teacher circulated the room asking questions such as: What do you think someone who wears a shoe like this is like as a person? What do you think they do for a job? How old do you think they are? Lively discussions – which went on as long as necessary – ensued. After this, pupils were given a picture of the *actual* wearer of the shoe and then made new inferences or built upon previous inferences. All the while, the teacher circulated and question-probed, constantly challenging pupils' thinking.

Next, pupils were given a piece of text written about the characters. For example, this was the text that accompanied a picture of a shoe worn by a man in a suit, typically corporate in appearance:

'He sat glumly on the sofa, head in his hands. It had been a long day; work was always stressful at this time of year. He heard a giggle from the kitchen. A smile crept across his face, remembering what, who, all the work was for. He stood up, walked into the kitchen, drawn by the sound. As he peered around the corner, a little hand waved towards him. His smile widened.'

Prior to reading the text, pupils inferred that this was a high-powered business type, but many changed their minds subsequently and imagined the wearer to be a tired, old dad. The teacher then posed the question: Why can't he be both? Again, lively discussion ensued.

Finally, pupils were given the choice to either write a character description or a diary entry – 'A day in the life of…' – for their respective characters, based upon all the information gathered as well as their own inferences.

No doubt you can identify lots of non-cognitive skills being utilised in Emily Weston's lesson.

It is worth noting that in education, the teacher must sometimes act as facilitator, like in the previous examples. At other times – like when I'm teaching about moles, concentration and volume – a teacher needs to stand at the front with nothing but a board marker and a cup of coffee and explain the shit out of something until it's fully understood. Stupid people often argue that a teacher's role must only be as a facilitator, and other equally stupid people argue the exact opposite. Anyone who still teaches, however, will tell you that both approaches are valid and it's your ability to effectively decide which approach to use and when to use it that makes you a good teacher. In short, don't feel obliged to use either method 100 per cent of the time.

One of the obstacles to overcome when trying to develop pupils' non-cognitive skills is that on the surface, it would appear that the curriculum does not lend itself to activities such as those described above as much as you would like. One way to overcome this is by remembering that, just like when you tell stories or 'bin the curriculum', you cannot do it all the time – ultimately, you don't decide the curriculum. But what you can do is inject this kind of lesson, for now, wherever is obvious (to you) and then gradually begin to seek out more opportunities. You'll have the knack of it in no time.

The other potential obstacle with these types of lessons is that they take longer to plan than normal. In this respect, it is even more important that you make sure your resources are as organised and reusable as possible. It is also a good idea to have a framework for such a lesson, which just needs adapting. The presentation for my fruit batteries lesson, for example, can be used for many other scientific – and even non-scientific – concepts. Perhaps find a framework you like and stick with it for a bit. You'll notice also that because non-cognitive skills are nurtured and not taught, these types of lessons don't require much teacher input. Where possible, then, save them for when the days are short, the nights are cold, the weather's crap and you're tired and stressed and haven't got the energy to stand at the front and bumble at a class that isn't even paying attention.

*

In conclusion, remember that no one is obliged to tell stories, 'bin the curriculum' or even develop non-cognitive skills beyond what is required of them. However, as a teacher, you have more opportunity to contribute to the holistic development of children – and therefore society at large – than you might imagine. Maximising on this opportunity would mean not only that pupils will be more enthused by your lessons, but also that they will leave school with more skills and become better-functioning adults.

And of course, it's those little things that they'll remember about your lessons in 20 years' time.

Summary

- Teachers – and others involved in education – often complain that the National Curriculum is too narrow in terms of the knowledge and skills that are taught. In places, it is also inaccessible.
- Assuming that pupils have no prior knowledge (and therefore recapping *everything*) will help to overcome the problem of inaccessibility. It will not take as long you imagine, but in any case it will save you time in the long run.
- You can enhance the curriculum somewhat by going slightly outside it and/or telling a personal story involving something from the lesson content. The key here is to seize any opportunity to make your lessons relevant to real life.
- The education system has a heavy focus on developing children's cognitive skills, whereas non-cognitive skills are developed incidentally. Non-cognitive skills, however, are just as essential in the long run. On occasion, try teaching your lessons in such a way that the development of non-cognitive skills is at the forefront. Create tasks that involve a lot of communication, collaboration, perseverance, self-management and creativity.

Chapter 4
How to overcome pupil apathy

One of the biggest shocks to the nervous system of new teachers is the lack of enthusiasm from many pupils. If you haven't already, you'll soon find yourself making a big deal out of a test for which only three pupils will bother to revise. You'll find yourself setting fun and engaging homework that three-quarters of the class won't do. You'll find yourself spending hours planning a lesson only for the class to interrupt you every 20 seconds. You'll find pupils being perfectly content with sub-standard grades and even failure. As the overwhelming majority of teachers had some intrinsic level of motivation when they were at school, it can be somewhat distressing to see their students waste such an important part of their lives.

By no means are all pupils apathetic, and the level of apathy – even in apathetic pupils – indeed varies. You may find some pupils highly enthusiastic in Year 7 and wholly disinterested in Year 11. You may find pupils who ignore you for two years and then start studying six weeks before the exam and get good grades. You may even find that a child who sits at the back of your room trying not to fall asleep behaves very differently in other subjects. Nonetheless, the problem of pupil apathy is significant and will likely be a key feature of your teaching career. The purpose of this chapter is neither to analyse the reasons nor to appoint blame for the former. Rather, as the pupils (and therefore their attitudes) play a key role in the education system, it is necessary for a teacher to know how to maximise their own influence.

The problems caused by apathy

The combination of pupil apathy and a target-driven system has led to a situation in which UK teachers do far more than what can be considered normal for a teacher elsewhere. It is common for intervention sessions for 'underachieving' pupils to take place before school, during lunchtimes and after school, and at some schools even during holidays and weekends. Generally speaking, the pupils who make the least amount of effort get a disproportionate amount of the teacher's time. No matter how much schools speak of maximising the individual capability of a child, you pretty much never see intervention taking place to get a child who is working on target above target.

As well as perpetual intervention, unfortunately the aforementioned combination has also driven many an educator (but still only a small minority) to commit malpractice. A brief internet search will lead you to numerous incidences of primary teachers explaining the question, giving clues, giving extra time and even outright giving away answers to pupils during SATs exams. In worst-case scenarios, papers have even been changed by senior leaders prior to being sent off. Similar happenings have occurred in secondary schools, where subject specialists 'somehow' ended up being in the exam hall with pupils or a headteacher took a handful of pupils out of the hall for a 'meeting'. In the latter cases, when coursework and controlled assessments still existed and were worth between 20 and 25 per cent of the GCSE grade, it wasn't uncommon for a pupil to get an A* in the coursework/controlled assessment, a D in the exam and therefore a C overall. Not-so-coincidentally, at the time, schools were judged by their percentage of five A*–C grades per pupil.

One by-product of apathy – although it is a bit chicken-and-eggish – is a sense of entitlement: that is, many pupils see their education as something that primarily has to be done by the teacher. Some entitled pupils will accuse teachers of not teaching properly or demand extra revision sessions despite making little effort themselves. Again, when you combine this with a target-driven system, you end up with schools that harness a 'customer's always right' approach, which disproportionately pressurises teachers. Is it a wonder, then, that employers complain about many school leavers' lack of initiative and need for very prescriptive instructions?

How to overcome pupil apathy

Be inspirational

I'm sure that your nan thinks you're inspirational, but there's a good chance that you probably aren't.

I'm kidding. Of course you are! But while you may well remember some of your own inspirational teachers, you probably can't put your finger on what exactly it was that made them inspirational.

A teacher's ability to inspire is due to a combination of their characteristics and actions. But before we go any further, let us be absolutely clear on one thing: there are literally tens of thousands of inspirational teachers, yet still far too many apathetic pupils. In other words, pupil apathy is not the fault of teachers, no matter how much some politicians may insist otherwise. As mentioned earlier, there are numerous reasons for pupil apathy, but analysing them is far beyond the scope of this book.

Nonetheless, it pays for a new teacher to know some of the things that inspirational teachers say and do that put them a cut above the rest to counter pupils' indifferent attitudes. Your good looks and dazzling personality aren't enough, I'm afraid.

Get your passion on

When you're passionate about something, rarely do you hide it: you raise your voice when you talk about it. You actively seek opportunities to talk about it. When other people talk about it, you jump into their conversation. You openly celebrate it. If you're lucky enough to have a classroom (yes, you read that correctly!), one way to show passion is by decorating it as if King Kong vomited your subject all over it. Use quotes, pupils' work, posters, 3D stuff – everything. While many contest the efficacy of classroom displays in terms of pupils' learning, they are still very much worth investing in because they raise the profile of a given subject/topic by making your passion prominent and visible.

Showing that you have passion – and therefore energy and enthusiasm – doesn't mean that you have to strut around your classroom with a permanent smile. It's fine if that's in your nature, but what will more effectively inspire your pupils is an open display of genuine enthusiasm for the subject matter. This can be difficult when you're teaching something for the fifteenth time, but there are key points in a lesson where simply changing your tone of voice will elicit a different response from pupils. No need to overdo it: kids recognise and don't respond well to fake behaviour. Just add a simple but genuine 'That's absolutely amazing, isn't it?' or something to that effect. You will no doubt have topics that you are more passionate about, so go all out when you're teaching those. In this context, it also helps to project your opinion onto pupils: 'One of the reasons why I studied XYZ at university was because I love this topic. I bet you will too.'

Depending on what you're teaching, you may have the golden opportunity to learn *with* your pupils. Not too long ago, I was teaching a lesson about the properties of carbon fibre. Instead of giving the kids laptops and asking them to do some research, I did a quick internet search and found the phone number of a manufacturer of carbon fibre bikes. I got the kids to think of some questions, put my mobile phone on speaker, got everyone quiet, dialled the number and asked the man what makes carbon fibre bikes so good. Apart from being a novel experience, pupils benefitted from seeing not only my enthusiasm for my subject, but also my enthusiasm for *learning* my subject. To be fair, I was genuinely impressed by the properties of carbon fibre!

If, for whatever reason, you can't get excited about the topic (this is perfectly normal for most non-robots), then get excited about achievement instead. For example, if you're teaching something like plant nutrients which irritates and bores the hell out of you, make a point of getting *extra* chuffed when your kids make progress or show a good level of understanding. Be careful, however, not to make a habit of over-praising, as it can encourage laziness. Remember that praise must be earned, but balance this with the need for a teacher to show overt enthusiasm in the lesson.

In terms of overcoming pupil apathy, the reason why a teacher's passion and enthusiasm are as important as their technical knowledge is because they are contagious: the more you have, the more your kids will have. It goes without saying, nonetheless, that kids will be kids, i.e. no matter how excited you are about the effects of magnesium on plants, pupils' enthusiasm will never match yours, and this is OK. The relationship is one of influence – not of balance – so what you do will inevitably make *some* difference.

Remember also that the way in which you show passion and enthusiasm is entirely your business. The signs may be more obvious in extroverted teachers, but don't assume that you have to go outside the parameters of your personality just because you have a subtler nature. As long as you are displaying what *you* consider to be signs, the kids will pick up on them and ultimately benefit.

Up your game

If you're a new teacher, there's a good chance that you will begin the profession less organised than even you – with all your highlighters, folders and planners – anticipated. No matter how high your level of planning and organisation, nothing prepares an NQT for a full teaching timetable. Luckily, any school worth teaching at is fully aware of this, so being behind on marking, teaching the wrong topic, teaching a bad lesson, etc. are all forgivable for a period of time. Depending on what stage in your career you're at when reading this, it may or may not fill you with joy to know that one of the main characteristics of inspirational teachers is that their lesson planning and general organisation are exceptional. It seems that the more you up your game, the more the kids up theirs.

Get your priorities straight

No doubt you will have been told to prioritise several times and are probably still trying to work out how (or are even beginning to doubt whether it's even possible!). Inspirational teachers prioritise two things. Firstly, they make sure that they teach good lessons – in the eyes of the pupils, that is. (Inspirational teachers are often mavericks who don't really care too much about school policy, etc. and get the job done in their own way, which pupils respond positively to.) Secondly, they prioritise the marking of assessments. Good lessons are obviously going to inspire, but it's easy for an adult to forget how frustrating it is for a child to wait for the results of an assessment. Even apathetic pupils want to know how they did, so by prioritising their marking, the message that you give pupils is that you care. Just like enthusiasm and passion, your caring attitude is also contagious: if you care, the kids are more likely to care. Every now and again, mark some tests ready for the next day/lesson, and when your kids are surprised, say, 'I couldn't wait to see how you did!' If they did poorly, tell them how upset you are that you made all this effort yet they couldn't even be bothered to revise. Nothing wrong with a bit of emotional blackmail.

Drop the act

New teachers – in fact, teachers full stop – are often told that 'teaching is an act'. While this is a good way to get teachers to maintain emotional control when dealing with pupil misbehaviour, as a statement in its own right it's not true – or at least it's not true for inspirational teachers. Inspirational teachers *feel* teaching, i.e. they consider it something beyond knowing a set of technical skills. They don't argue much over pedagogy; rather, they firmly espouse the view that if it works for you in your classroom, do it! Teaching is a part of their personhood; they embrace who they are. They only act when they need to and the resulting authenticity means that everything they say and do has the power to stick. So if you want to be inspirational, save the acting for when a wasp comes into your classroom during period 5 on a Friday.

Get your GRIT on

There is *a part* of even the most apathetic pupil that *does* care about their education. If their apathy went to the core, they wouldn't try to look at their reports before their parents/guardians saw them; they wouldn't get annoyed if you made them wait five weeks for the results of a test; and the novelty of having a supply teacher wouldn't wear off after three days. What teachers find perplexing, however, is that while pupils have the desire for a good academic outcome, too many do not have the 'grit' necessary to attain it.

Psychologist Angela Lee Duckworth defines 'grit' as *passion* and sustained *persistence* applied towards long-term achievement, with no particular concern for rewards or recognition along the way. It combines resilience, ambition and self-control in the pursuit of short- or long-term goals. Duckworth's study of 'grit' began when she worked as a teacher and realised that IQ wasn't the only factor determining a child's academic success: 'grit', too, was a strong predictor. Much like the non-cognitive skills mentioned in Chapter 3, grit cannot outright be taught. If we want 'gritty' kids, we have to nurture and encourage 'grit' in the classroom.

There is no reason why you can't show Duckworth's viral TED Talk on 'grit' to your class, particularly if there are a substantial number of pupils who want good results but don't want to do the work. It would make for a good discussion about how, in life, one rarely gets something for nothing and how pretty much anybody whom the pupils would consider a role model will have endured significant hardship in order to achieve a goal. This is also a good chance for you to sell the idea of education to pupils, i.e. its benefits in terms of the wider impact on society that you can have as an educated person, as well as better employment prospects.

Pupils often give up when a task is 'too hard'. It is common for new (or even experienced) teachers to rush in and give help, scaffold, etc. before the child has been given the chance to apply any 'grit' that they may possess. With much help from the teacher, they eventually get the answer, everyone's happy and the class moves on. I'm convinced that for most teachers it's our saviour complex that makes us help the child too soon. So, while we can't blame ourselves entirely, if we want to encourage 'grit', we have to do things a little bit differently.

Instead of jumping in immediately, then, get pupils to stay with the pain, so to speak, by shifting your focus from the outcome to the *process*. Let's say that your class is about to start a challenging task. Instead of promising a reward to the one who finishes first, try telling them something to the effect of: 'I don't care if it's wrong at this stage. I want to see you trying your best to follow the method. With a task like XYZ, it's perfectly normal to get it wrong a few times before you get it right.' Unless it's group work, insist on pin-drop silence. Don't walk around the room (kids will ask for help if you do). Don't check your emails either. Instead, watch your class from the front and if anyone's looking around, whispering, etc., get them back on task however you normally would. By shifting your focus, the message that you're giving pupils is that while the process may hurt, it is necessary and the ability to endure it is on par with the outcome itself. Also, by outright telling pupils that a wrong answer is common, you are removing the negative connotations associated with failure, hence better enabling your pupils to engage with difficulty.

Doesn't it do your head in when you've just explained a concept, checked that your class understood it and then handed out some questions, only within seconds to be bombarded with:

'I don't get it!'

'It doesn't make sense!'

'Sir/Miss, this is too hard!'

'I can't do it!'

To encourage 'grit', then, why not create a list of 'forbidden phrases'? Have phrases like the above on your wall, crossed out perhaps. Instead of vague statements like 'It doesn't make sense', encourage pupils to ask specific questions *about* the questions that they're stuck on. If the question is 'Why is the grass under the rabbit hutch yellow?' for example, and the child doesn't know the answer, a 'gritty' question from them may be 'Can the rabbit get out of the hutch?', as it shows that they are thinking about possible reasons *before* asking. (By the way, it's because photosynthesis can't take place as the hutch is blocking the sunlight. Not because the rabbit weed on it.)

And finally, refer to famous gritty people. As well as sports heroes, use actors, singers and anyone else popular among the youth. The latter two are not seen as particularly 'gritty' in the way that sports heroes are, so when you share their stories you're guaranteed to see your pupils' eyes light up. Tales of repeated failure/rejection followed by success are the most effective because, sadly, too many children believe that you either are or aren't 'clever'. In other words, many believe that their role models are *entirely* a product of natural talent. I know that I was a kid like that! I recall being in shock when my English teacher told me that Stephen King was rejected by multiple publishers and when my A level chemistry teacher told me that he failed his A levels the first time. Funny how I remember these not-so-minor details but I don't remember them referring to my 'target grade' or 'predicted grade' even once. Bizarre, right?

The opposite of apathy

Another issue with the education system is that it produces many pupils who see education as a series of exams that have to be passed in order to attain a career. In other words, pupils see education as a selfish endeavour and teachers, through no fault of our own, perpetuate this view.

As apathetic pupils receive a disproportionate amount of the teacher's time, and kids being on or above target is never going to be considered a bad thing, rarely does a teacher stop and think about the implications of the 'exam-passing' culture of which we are very much a part.

Ironically, the education system does not emphasise the importance of an education. Yes, it improves one's life chances overall, but an equally important reason to receive an education is (or at least should be) to put oneself in a better position to positively influence society. Directly or indirectly, people have to benefit from educated people.

Currently, the focus on achievement is far greater than the focus on purpose. One can't help but wonder why, then, some of the worst corporate crimes have been committed by the world's most educated people: toxic mortgages issued by Ivy League university graduates played a massive role in the 2008 global credit crunch, and the people at the heart of the scandals of WorldCom, Enron and dozens of others were of the same ilk. Of course, it would be both absurd and incorrect to argue that all of these crimes were committed solely because the teachers of those involved gave them too many past papers in the lead-up to their exams when they were at school. Obviously not. But one can't help but wonder whether if the *purpose* of education was as emphasised as the *achievement* of education, the system would be more likely to produce better people? When we tell our pupils that they have to get their grades no matter what, and don't give them any reason beyond their own lives/careers as to why, should we be surprised when some of them later grow into selfish adults? Perhaps if we told our children that an education will help them to change the world for the better – like the scientists of the Middle Ages, for example – they'd develop into far more altruistic adults.

By all means, continue to get your pupils to reach their full academic potential. Just be sure to tell them why.

Summary

- While it varies from school to school, generally speaking, pupil apathy is a common problem for teachers.
- Pupil apathy is one of the reasons for excessive academic intervention by teachers, which can lead to a sense of entitlement from pupils.
- One way to help overcome pupil apathy is by being an inspirational teacher. Inspirational teachers show passion (through their energy and enthusiasm), are well organised (as can be seen in their planning and marking) and are genuine in their interactions with pupils.
- Apathetic pupils are often lacking in 'grit' (sustained perseverance). You can develop 'grit' in your pupils by not being too quick to provide support with difficult tasks and by encouraging them to 'stay with the pain'. Creating a list of forbidden phrases can help with this.
- The opposite of an apathetic pupil is a pupil who views education as a selfish endeavour. If we want our children to develop into altruistic adults, we have to teach them that the purpose of education is to put oneself in a better position to bring about positive change for the world.

Chapter 5
How to make paper *work*

One of the biggest problems that teachers – particularly new teachers – face is the unparalleled level of bureaucracy and accountability a teaching career entails. Whether it's lesson observations, learning walks or book scrutinies, a teacher is always in a position where they are having to prove themselves, in one way or another. In this chapter we will explore the different types of bureaucracy and accountability (which have collectively been dubbed 'paperwork' due to the large amounts of paper, time and energy that they involve), as well as some strategies for how best to deal with them.

The problem with paperwork

The main reason for paperwork is commonly perceived to be a lack of professional trust. For one reason or another (these would require an entirely separate book to explore in full), the government just does not trust teachers to adequately do what they are passionate about. They don't trust us to teach properly so they keep observing us. They don't trust us to give verbal feedback – despite it being more effective – so they make us waste hours a week on written feedback. To put it bluntly, whatever you *say* you do as a teacher doesn't mean diddly-squat: your teaching ability will be judged by what can be *proven*. The absolute worst thing about bureaucracy is actually not the fact that it is rooted in distrust. Rather, one major complaint from teachers is that the time spent ticking somebody else's boxes and jumping through hoops is time that could have been spent making themselves better teachers or otherwise positively impacting their pupils. If you didn't laugh you'd cry.

While the level of bureaucracy varies from school to school, it is very much here to stay. Veteran teachers can tell you about education secretary after education secretary promising a reduction thereof but, more often than not, they either do nothing or replace one form of bureaucracy with another.

The above might not exactly fill you with joy. Remember, however, that many a teacher remains happy in the profession in spite of this, and if you're clever about it, you can get through much of the bureaucratic stuff without it catching you out, stressing you out or otherwise wasting more time than necessary.

How to make paper *work*

Observations

One would hope that after a rigorous training year, lesson observations would quickly become a thing of the past. Sadly, this is not the case: while the frequency and nature of lesson observations is very much dependent upon how your school is led, your teaching *will* be assessed throughout your career. With the right finesse, however, you can get through a lesson observation with relative ease.

Get your attitude right

You'll be relieved to know that while the observation process is always somewhat stressful, it gets significantly easier with experience, and any teacher who has had an observation disaster most probably had it in their early years of teaching, after which they fully 'recovered'. There is, of course, no shame in this, as by definition NQTs are inexperienced and mistakes are inevitable. Nonetheless, it is more than possible to get it right the first time.

As a new teacher establishing yourself, your attitude towards an observation is going to count for as much as the observation itself. By this, what I mean is that some NQTs may underperform in an NQT observation because they unwittingly treat them the same way in which they (rightly) treated their early PGCE observations, i.e. as developmental – to learn and improve from. Don't get me wrong, NQT observations usually *are* developmental as well, but the difference is that the developmental aspect of the observation exists within a narrower parameter. In other words, the observer will be more focused on *assessing* your teaching than they would be during the early stages of the PGCE. In this respect, then, it is essential to show an attitude of wanting to succeed. Following the remaining guidance in this section will help to ensure this but, in addition, make it obvious that you know you are being assessed: 'I want them to see me at my best' is what your attitude must convey. Get your lesson plan checked well in advance, and don't go panic-printing or panic-marking on the morning of your observation (not that you would have done this on your PGCE, but in the NQT year, it is important that you treat the observation like a test that needs passing). When your observer(s) see(s) your attitude, they will subconsciously hold you in high regard, even before the observation begins.

Plan in detail

Your school will no doubt have a lesson-planning proforma upon which you have to… wait for it… plan your lesson. It goes without saying that this is the one that you have to use – not the one you acquired from the TES last year. Schools want nothing more than to believe that they are unique and innovative, so don't go kicking up a stink by using some other school's 'inferior' proforma. What schools don't really do, however, is tell you the level of detail to go into when writing your lesson plan.

Generally speaking, the less experience you have, the more detailed your lesson plan should be, and there are two reasons for this. Firstly, as an NQT, you are an unknown quantity, i.e. you have yet to prove yourself before anyone knows you're a good teacher. In this spirit, then, the more that you can show your observers how much you thought about your lesson (remember, thoughts are not visible until they're written), the more conscientious a teacher you will appear. Secondly, if your lesson doesn't go as well as you anticipated, be assured that your planning will be closely scrutinised during the feedback; the discussion will be a whole lot easier if your plan is right in front of you. Put *everything* on the plan. You may know full well what you mean when you say 'go through answers' but your observer doesn't. Instead, write something to the effect of: 'Use targeted questioning to elicit responses from high prior attaining pupils (Tom, Imran, Kate) and only show mark scheme answers after snowballing has taken place'. Catch my drift?

Don't put on a show

While your attitude must be positive and your planning detailed, you must not – or even appear to – put on a show. A 'show' can be best illustrated by example. A teacher who was known for regularly coming late to school, being on her phone at inappropriate times and giving book-work far more often than what was normal for most teachers was once given five working days' notice for an observation. Immediately, she began printing off exam-style questions from parts of the shared area that she never previously knew existed. She tidied her room, used a guillotine to make card sorts and even wrote a five-page lesson plan, despite never having been seen with her teacher planner prior to this. On paper, her lesson plan would've been considered 'outstanding', but within moments of entering the room, the observers could see that the entire charade was exactly that. While their professional instincts and evidence gathered from numerous learning walks was enough to tell them that it was a farce, what confirmed their beliefs was the testimony of the pupils when they asked them, 'How does this lesson compare to normal lessons?' To add insult to an inevitable injury, the teacher had given six books – brilliantly marked according to school policy – to the observers as examples of her marking at the start of the lesson. Can you guess what the observers did after looking at those six pristine books? Yup, you got it in one: they checked the rest of the books and found that they hadn't been marked for several weeks.

Obviously, if you were as incompetent as the aforementioned teacher, you probably wouldn't bother reading an education book. Nonetheless, I'm sure you take the point from the extreme example.

'When you've got guests, you tidy up. You don't buy new furniture,' was what a deputy head once told staff before an observation cycle. Nothing could be truer: during an observation, you want to exaggerate and make obvious *what you normally do*, in terms of both your attitude and the content of your lesson. If you're reading this as a new teacher, don't panic – it is perfectly normal to not have absolute confidence in what you 'normally do' (yet) as it is, of course, still undergoing development. Think of the observation as a chance to show the *best* of what you normally do.

Make it obvious

Like every school, yours too will have taken on some sort of initiative that requires you to include certain activities and/or address particular skills in your lessons. It is in areas such as these where the need to make them obvious both on your lesson plan *and* in your lesson is somewhat greater. Whether it's your NQT mentor or a senior member of staff, the observer will need to be certain that whole-school initiatives are being acted upon. Fortunately, it doesn't have to be onerous. A simple 'Right, kids, if you've finished, move on to the LITERACY TASK!' should do the trick. Think of it like the driving test: when you normally check your rear-view mirror, you probably do it without moving your head. Before your test, however, your instructor would most probably have told you to raise your head slightly. Apply the same logic to a lesson observation.

At the time of writing, one of the key measures for the success of a lesson is the progress made by the pupils in a given period of time, usually around 30 minutes. In this spirit, as well as what can be deduced from the driving test analogy, make sure that you can answer two questions when planning your lesson:

1   How will I know that pupils have learned?

2   Can I prove it?

Oftentimes, us teachers, rightly or wrongly, rely on our gut instincts to tell us whether or not pupils understand a particular concept, whether it's OK to move on, etc. Having 15 years' experience, I can often tell whether or not something needs re-explaining simply by the way in which the class is looking at me. A couple of questions targeted to a couple of pupils is literally enough for me to know whether or not it's OK to move on. In a lesson observation (and this is the main reason why they piss me off), it's not just me that has to know – it's also the observer. In this case, I might question-probe more frequently – even if I'm certain that the pupils know it – or I may ask a pupil to repeat the explanation that I've just given when I know they understood it the first time. In short, make sure that learning is taking place (obviously) *and is easily observable* to whoever comes into your room and starts poking around for evidence of progress.

Do as you're told... but not always

It isn't uncommon for schools – particularly those that are part of multi-academy trusts – to insist that their teachers plan lessons using a very rigid format. You might, for example, *have* to recap prior learning at the start of a lesson and follow it immediately by direct instruction. You may *have* to display a picture on the screen and ask pupils to guess what the lesson's going to be about. Whatever your school prescribes, the issue is usually not whether or not it is good practice as, more often than not, it is. The problem is that not everything you teach will lend itself to the way in which they want you to teach it. This can be frustrating for some teachers because, as well as feeling like you're being dictated to, you sometimes feel like you are compelled to ignore common sense and do what has to be done, rather than what works. Some teachers will ignore whole-school instructions and do as they please (and then panic when they have an observation), while others will stress themselves out by doing everything by the book. Savvy teachers will do what their SLTs ask, but will happily turn away from their guidelines if necessity dictates otherwise. When it comes to the observation, then, the kids will at least be familiar with the prescribed format/activities and so the lesson will be successful.

All about assessment?

While lesson observations are often about assessing the teacher, by no means is this always the case. Many schools acknowledge the value in teachers observing teachers and therefore arrange or encourage 'buddy' observations. If you are taking part in these or something similar, it is no longer necessary to play it safe in the way that this section suggests. The whole purpose is to be daring so, absolutely, do something you've never done before! It goes without saying, nonetheless, that the moment someone is watching, some level of judgement is inevitably being made. In other words, while you may decide to get your kids to make up a rap about photosynthesis, be mindful of the fact that if your books aren't marked or the class's behaviour has dipped, well, it will be noticed. So again, tidy up (a little bit) before these. If you're an NQT, observing a variety of teachers will do no end of good for your teaching, so make sure that you get observing lessons even if you have not been explicitly told to do so. If you know of particular teachers who are good in areas in which you need further development, for example, there is no harm in asking them whether you can drop in some time. (Wait until they give you a date and time, though – don't just go showing up randomly!)

Also, as an NQT, you will likely be encouraged to have informal observations throughout the year. It is in your best interests to take advantage of these, not only because they make a formal observation a lot more bearable, but also because it is one of the best ways to improve your teaching: people improve in an environment in which they are encouraged to learn from – rather than fear – mistakes. Make a point of requesting an observation with your mentor (or anyone else with whom you feel relaxed, comfortable and not judged by) wherever possible. By all means do it to show off your best stuff – it's nice being told where your strengths lie – but also ask the observer to focus particularly on areas that you suspect may be weaker.

Book scrutinies

Book look. Book check. Feedback analysis. Whatever a school decides to call it, the purpose of it is universally the same: to ensure that your books are marked in accordance with school policy. Just like lesson observations and learning walks, school leaders will extrapolate the findings of a book scrutiny – i.e. if your observed lesson is poor, they will assume that your normal teaching is poor; if they check a sample of your books and you haven't marked them, they will assume that you haven't marked the rest either. Luckily, in both situations the first thing that senior leaders will do is give you a chance to redeem yourself through a re-observation or a request for more books. While they can be quite daunting in your early years of teaching, if you form the right habits from the start, a book scrutiny can be a breeze.

As good teachers tend to prioritise lesson planning over marking, it is almost inevitable that marking – and the condition of pupils' exercise books generally – is the thing that teachers, through no real fault of our own, let slip. While book scrutiny tick lists will vary from school to school, they will generally be looking for three things:

1   that the type and frequency of marking/feedback is in accordance with school policy

2   that books are as well presented as is reasonably possible

3   that the books contain sufficient evidence of what goes on in the lesson.

We can tackle these one by one.

Make it obvious

The first point is a no-brainer: mark your books the way in which you're told. It is worth noting, however, that because schools rarely make their staff mark everything in books, what you *do* mark must stand out. Let's say, for example, that you decided to mark a homework sheet that you asked pupils to stick in their books. It may sound trivial, but make sure that the sheet is not folded when it's stuck in! You see, whoever is checking your books will probably have 500 other things that they could be doing, so the last thing they will want to do is spend ages unfolding sheets or otherwise going on a wild goose chase for marked work. Whatever your policy, make it obvious that you're following it. Don't go hiding your marking or writing comments in a place where an observer will struggle to see them. Remember the driving test?

Book tidy

The second request is a bit more difficult to manage, as it involves getting pupils to do something and not you. New teachers often expect the pupils they teach to be as conscientious as they were when they were at school, and it's not until they collect books in for the first time that they realise pupils haven't stuck sheets in despite being told several times, they haven't used rulers to underline despite being told several times and they haven't written the date despite being told several times. Don't get me wrong, every teacher goes around their class to check books, but you're (rightly) more interested in how much work they've done, whether they need help, etc. Unless you're a neatness freak, you probably couldn't give a shit if a sheet is left unstuck, and this is OK in the short term. One way to avoid a book-scrutiny panic is by having a 'book tidy' every few lessons, and particularly before the scrutiny. All you have to do is hand out glue (if your school is lucky enough to have some!), pencils and rulers and go around the class making sure that pupils spend the five allocated minutes doing exactly that. Try to encourage pupils to get it right the first time, but even if you don't, the majority of pupils will get the idea after the 53rd book tidy.

Signpost

School leaders will use pupils' books to get at least an inkling of what goes on in the lesson. In this respect, the more that you can spell it out the better. Many schools request that teachers do this anyway, but as it's not onerous, you might as well get the pupils to signpost regardless, i.e. write SA in the margin when they've done self-assessment, PA for peer-assessment, Lit. for literacy and/or whatever else is necessary to show that you are following whole-school policy in your daily practice.

And finally, if you're a new teacher or a teacher new to a particular school, it is perfectly acceptable to ask someone 'above' you, or even a fellow teacher, to have a quick flick through a couple of your books prior to the scrutiny just to be certain. Unfortunately, at times, the system happily tells you what you're doing wrong without first having told you how to get it right. Also, in this spirit, it is perfectly acceptable to ask to see the book scrutiny checklist – the one used by the checkers – well before any scrutiny. Most schools are fine with this, but you'll be surprised how many get all secretive!

Performance management

After your NQT year, you will be subjected to a performance management process that has the main purpose of ensuring and enabling a teacher's professional development. In recent years, however, it has also become increasingly necessary to pass performance management targets in order to progress up the pay-scale. In light of both of these things – but particularly the latter – it is important to get it right lest you end up living with your parents forever. While there are subtle differences across schools, performance management processes are essentially the same: targets are set and if you meet them, you pass your performance management. If you don't, you won't necessarily fail, but passing becomes a bit more difficult. In either case, you will have to provide evidence of both meeting the target and any action taken to meet the target.

There are usually between three and four targets. Some are agreed between you and your line manager, and others are given to you. Most of the time there will be:

- a numerical target, e.g. 50 per cent of class 11X1 to achieve one grade above expected
- a teaching target, e.g. develop the use of oracy activities in lessons
- a curriculum development target, e.g. to contribute to the development of the new Year 8 scheme of work.

When a target is outright given to you, it's probably whole-school so you don't really have a say in it. Where there is leeway, however, it is wise to choose something that is going to make passing performance management easier. Don't go making your life unnecessarily difficult! For example, let's say that the numerical target can be set by you with a group chosen by you. In this situation, pick a reasonable target with a group with which you feel you are likely to succeed. This might be obvious to some, but in the early years of teaching, your energy is disproportionately spent (rightly so) on finding your feet in the classroom, and so it's easy to end up agreeing to something without having first thought it through. The same applies to other targets: make a conscious effort to choose either something that you are *already doing* and want to do better or something that you know you will be successful in doing. No doubt some will be dismayed by my advice and accuse me of lowering teachers' aspirations. For those people, all I will say is that there are literally hundreds of other ways in which you can be aspirational and I very much encourage you to be! Performance management is by no means the only opportunity for professional development, and no reasonable person can fault a teacher for exercising caution where their pay progression is concerned.

As the daily grind of teaching is so intense, it is not uncommon for newish teachers to put their performance management targets on the back-burner and then run around like headless chickens two weeks before the deadline, thinking, 'Shit. What were my targets again? Where's my evidence?!' It is important, then, that once you are clear on the evidence requirements, you collect this as you go along. Saving particular emails in a particular folder or having a performance management evidence folder on your desktop will save you a lot of time and headaches.

If it is self-evident that you have achieved a target, e.g. 50 per cent of the class did indeed achieve above expected, then performance management reviewers are less fussed about what you did and how you did it, so if you ever need to prioritise, put this at the bottom of your list. It's when you *don't* achieve a target that evidence becomes of paramount importance. Now let me repeat: not achieving one target is not the end of the world. A lot of schools will have a 'partially met' box, and many will award some kind of credit to a teacher who has at least *tried* to achieve a target, on the condition, of course, that they can prove it. The key thing here is to anticipate. That is, if you fear that you may not meet a target, do something about it early. If it's a numerical target then, in addition to employing the strategies for managing data mentioned in Chapter 6, make a concerted effort to make sure that your line manager is fully aware of exactly what you are doing to make sure the target *is* met. Speak to them in person (preferably) or fire a quick email.

In the event of you not meeting a target, it is not only important that you have the necessary evidence to prove what actions you took, but it is also a good idea to go slightly above and beyond in this instance. By this, I mean that your school will already have some basic requirement for evidence but, to strengthen your case, don't be afraid to go outside of this. For example, I once taught a class who, for various reasons, were destined to achieve poor results. While they were at best compliant in the classroom, no matter what I did, they did not revise or otherwise take an interest in the subject. When it finally came to performance management, their results were indeed as poor as I had expected, but luckily I was to have two saving graces. Firstly, I decided to hand out pupil voice surveys to the pupils, in essence to ask them what they thought about my teaching. My plan was to either show my reviewer how good my teaching was (hey, come on – you've got to blow your own trumpet every now and then) or tell my reviewer what I would do differently next time, thereby showing what an excellent reflective practitioner I was. Secondly, as the TA in my lessons always commented on how she'd never seen these kids behaving so well, I asked her to send me a short email outlining what she'd seen in my lessons. This and the pupil voice surveys were glowing. I took them both to the performance management meeting and they did more than compensate for the students' poor results. It goes without saying that the stringency of performance management requirements varies from school to school, but in this respect, doing that little bit extra will always help you and never harm you. Be proactive, not reactive.

As well as getting evidence from novel sources, be extra thorough with the required evidence. So if, let's say, you had to provide details of an intervention that you put in place, make sure that you state the topics that you chose to cover as well as *why* you chose them.

It is worth noting that it is easier to get through performance management in the earlier years of your career. The more years you've been teaching, the higher your salary gets and the more difficult it gets to pass performance management. Being savvy to the process in your early years of teaching will pay no end of dividends further down the line.

Summary

- Teaching is high in bureaucracy and accountability – paperwork. It is commonly believed that excessive paperwork is rooted in professional distrust. Due to its time-consuming nature, paperwork, ironically, can be detrimental to a teacher's practice.
- The main paperwork-heavy tasks are lesson observations, book scrutinies and performance management. (There are others, of course, such as report writing, but they are less frequent and less under the control of teachers.)
- Successful observations are the result of a positive attitude *before* the observation as well as meticulous planning, an elaborate adherence to whole-school policy and tangible progress being evident. You should exaggerate the best of what you normally do and never put on a show. If you're a new teacher, take full advantage of informal observations.
- The key to a successful book scrutiny is to make everything obvious, i.e. make sure that your marking stands out and your pupils have signposted. Make time for 'book tidies' every so often, as neglecting books is inevitable.
- After your NQT year, you will be subject to performance management reviews, which essentially consist of three or four targets, some of which are chosen by you while others are decided by school leaders. Choose your targets wisely. Moving up the pay-scale is increasingly dependent upon passing performance management targets but there is wriggle room. Collecting evidence as you go along will prevent panic later on. Evidence is more important when proving what you did to *try to meet a target you haven't met* than when you've actually met a target.

Chapter 6
How to manage all things data

At some point in your life, no doubt, some smart alec has tried to explain something difficult to you – a scientific concept, the details of a political situation or even just how to work the TV remote. How annoying did you find it when they kept asking, 'Do you get it? Don't you get it? Why don't you get it?' If the education system was a person, that's exactly the person it would be: the annoying know-it-all who keeps testing people, probably to make themselves feel better due to some deep-seated insecurity.

While the education system may not be an actual person, the described nature of its character is not entirely hyperbolic: the education system, and therefore schools, is and are incapable of just leaving teachers be. To be absolutely blunt, the measurement of pupil – and therefore teacher – progress is relentless and is a very real source of stress for teachers and pupils alike.

Once we know what to expect from the education system, however, there is much that we can do to better manage all things data and make this potentially disheartening part of the system work better for us and our pupils.

The problem with data

As a teacher, you are expected to regularly assess your pupils, derive grades/percentages for these assessments and enter them into some sort of digital application at regular intervals throughout the school year. In addition, you will be expected to explain the data – for which you are highly accountable – during progress meetings, which usually follow data-entry points.

While schools may choose to call them by different names, every school will have some version of (and accompanying problems with) current grades and target grades.

Current grades

A school report normally requires that you state a child's current grade in a particular subject. This may seem simple enough, but in actual fact, it is a perpetual source of confusion. The word 'current' can mean many things. Is it the grade that they would get if they were to sit the exam right now? Surely that would be a fail because not even half the content has been covered by the first data drop? Or is it the grade that they would get if they continued to work at the same level? In that case, surely the content will become more difficult? How then do you know that they will continue to work at the same level?

Aside from the aforementioned confusion that almost certainly accompanies a data drop, the other issue with current grades is that they are collected too frequently. Assuming that you can ascribe a 'correct' current grade in the first instance, it won't be long before you're asked for a current grade again. The system tends to want to measure progress before the time necessary to make said progress has passed. Not only that, but schools only recognise one type of progress – linear progress – and for the reporting system, this means that pupils are not allowed to 'go backwards', i.e. if their previous current grade was a 5, then rarely to never are you allowed to put it down to a 4 for the next data point, *even if* they have underperformed in assessments since then. Anyone who has learned to drive, learned a language or simply been alive for any length of time knows that progress, in anything, is almost never 100 per cent linear. Rather, progress is made *overall* but there are peaks and troughs along the way. A current grade, then, is at worst false, and at best waffly.

Target grades

You've probably gathered by now that every student at more or less every stage in their compulsory education is assigned a target grade. While in theory it makes perfect sense to have a goal to work towards – consciously or unconsciously, we all do it – the reality is, well, a little harsh.

As target grades are often portrayed as the expectation of pupils (some schools even outright call them 'expected' grades), a new teacher may wrongly assume that the target grade is perfectly reasonable and easily within a child's reach. The reality, however, is that target grades are in fact aspirational, i.e. achieving them requires a special effort from you and your pupils; their attainment is not a given. Obviously, you'd make a special effort for your pupils regardless, but know that, generally speaking, if you were to ask ten teachers about target grades, nine of them would tell you that often, but not always, they're too high. The reason for this is that in secondary schools, for example, target grades are based on Key Stage 2 SATs results for English and maths. As mentioned in Chapter 3, a whole lot of prep goes into the SATs, so naturally the grades are higher than they would otherwise be. High grades mean high targets and, to add insult to injury, the target grades for a given subject are often not based on a pupil's prior attainment in that very subject. So, pupils could very easily be targeted a high grade in secondary science, for example, solely because their Key Stage 2 attainment in English and maths was high. Lest we wrongly appoint blame, it is worth noting that Key Stage 2 targets are decided using equally arbitrary methods, i.e. targets are decided by achievement in the previous stage.

And that's just the obvious problem. Unfortunately, target grades also come with some potentially serious consequences. Where a pupil is not on track to achieve a target grade, for example, the resulting pressure on teachers can cause unreasonable levels of stress, which itself can adversely affect pupils. In addition, some type of teacher intervention becomes necessary, and all too often the child – who may genuinely be trying their best – ends up feeling like they're stupid. In secondary schools, 'underachieving' pupils will simultaneously have their subject teacher, form tutor and head of house constantly telling them that they're underachieving and must do XYZ about it. If laziness is the cause, well, that's different, but if not, the system is responsible for damaging a lot of kids' self-esteem, irrespective of how gentle their school's approach to intervention may be.

As well as making the notion of progress feel like some obscure possibility, target grades also have the power to do the exact opposite: limit success. It is perfectly possible for a pupil to be assigned a target grade that you know is far too low for their ability – or at least your perception thereof. But because the system drills the importance of achieving target grades into children from a very young age, often what happens is that pupils who could probably do even better limit their effort and therefore their own progress. It is natural for kids, particularly teenagers, to take the path of least resistance and do the bare minimum required of them, but it is wrong for the education system to enable this.

How to manage all things data

An alternative message

No matter what your opinions on target grades, the simple fact is that if pupils don't achieve them, you will, as a minimum, have to prove that you did everything in your power to ensure that they would. So how, then, do we balance the need to achieve targets with some of the issues described so far?

Granted, targets may be arbitrary, too high, too low, limit success or ruin self-esteem, but what will make the greatest difference to pupils achieving or even exceeding them is how much effort they put in. Employment – and indeed life full stop – requires GRIT, so the best thing that we can do for our pupils is to encourage them to do their best while at the same time making them aware that *their best is good enough*. Instead of repeatedly banging on about target grades or otherwise giving pupils the impression that their existence is validated by their achievement (there was once a school that had the kids' pictures and target grades literally hanging from the ceiling of the classroom), try saying:

'Your target is to do your best.'

Whenever you discuss target grades with your class, throw in and really emphasise the above statement – feel free to add some more teacher rap to it. By encouraging effort, we not only help pupils to reach their full academic potential, but we also remove some of the aforementioned issues arising from target grades.

Absorb the pressure

It goes without saying that we cannot ignore target grades completely, and even the alternative message above must be given *as well as* – not instead of – everything else that you say. In your lessons, then, it is important that you are reminding pupils of their target grades as well as making sure that current grade/target grade stickers on books, etc. are all up to date. Much of this will most probably be school policy anyway, but as the education system is so data-driven, it is worth emphasising the point again.

As mentioned earlier, this part of the system has the potential to cause a lot of anxiety for teachers, which can have reverberating affects. New teachers: there's a good chance that you've had the experience of leaving your starter activity at the photocopier and beginning your lesson in a flustered state to a bunch of kids who don't seem to want to be quiet. The more visibly irate you became, the noisier they got. The noisier they got, the more visibly irate you became. You know how it ends.

Managing data is no different to managing behaviour: the more anxiety you show, the more your lack of certainty will cause your pupils to act up. When managing target grades, then, don't allow pupils to *notice* or *catch* your anxiety (anxiety is contagious) by showing them any signs of it. In other words, you cannot appear stressed about pupils who are off target.

Firstly, doing so doesn't work anyway – all it does is undermine you. If you teach secondary and you appear stressed, the kids may outright take the piss: 'Let's fail so that Miss doesn't get paid!' In any case, you're doing a disservice to your pupils if you openly take responsibility for something that they are ultimately responsible for and not you – probably not a good message to give to people who will soon enough be in employment.

Secondly, there is the risk of blowback: if you teach at a leafy green suburban school, you may well miss out on the low-level disruption and violence common at inner city schools, but this will very probably be replaced by some over-protective, mollycoddling parents. So if little Percy decides that you're stressing him out, his parents will be on the phone to your line manager. As well as being prone to catching stress, Percy-type pupils have a tendency to deflect pressure. Let's say that you stressed Percy out for not achieving his target grade. Percy will go home and tell his parents – who are also pressuring him to achieve his target – that the reason he's not is because you're not teaching him properly. They will be on the phone.

To avoid the above, then, it is important that you absorb the pressure and instead use the motivation and inspiration strategies described in Chapter 4. By all means, tell your pupils off when they're being lazy and put a reasonable amount of pressure on them, but avoid anything that would indicate that it's *you* that's stressed. By and large, kids have good intuition, so if ever your responses are overly emotional they will feed off them. Instead, be theatrical at all times and always remember that there is only so much you can do.

On a side note, notice that I'm only discouraging the *display* of stress/anxiety and not judging those who experience stress/anxiety. Within parameters, stressing about pupils' lack of achievement is perfectly normal for most teachers. Save the rants for the pub or, if you feel that you are unable to manage your stress levels, seek support and/or make any changes to your life that would improve your wellbeing.

How to use target grades in your lessons

To repeat, many pupils will limit their effort – and therefore their success – the moment that they are satisfied that their target grade has been achieved. If ever there was a definition of counterproductive, it is this. We may not like the concept of target grades, but there're a couple of things that we can do to make sure they don't backfire.

During your teacher training, during an INSET or during whatever, you may have been taught to set graded tasks, i.e. starting off easy and then getting harder, and to make all tasks available to all pupils. There is, of course, nothing wrong with this and in my opinion it's actually good practice. The potential problems, however, arise when you ascribe grades to the tasks *and make pupils aware of them.* Let's say, for example, that task A is a grade 4, task B a 5, and task C a 6. A student fitting the aforementioned description will likely get to task B and think, 'Well, I've already got my target grade,' and then start talking to the person next to them. While such a task is not being dismissed as bad practice necessarily (although some in the edusphere consider it impossible to appoint grades to skills/content in this way), why not give this a try: do the exact same thing as above but, this time, omit the grades from the task. Do what you would normally do – motivate pupils, provide scaffolding, etc. – but don't tell them the grade until either they've completed the task or you are satisfied with the level of effort that they've made. Both you and your pupils will be surprised at what they are capable of when the aim of the task shifts from attainment to understanding. (Not that the two aren't related, of course.) Since the curriculum changed, as described in

Chapter 3, once my pupils have understood difficult concepts, I make a point of telling them, 'This is also on the A level spec.' Call me sad, but to this day, I feel warm and fuzzy inside when I see how visibly chuffed they get. Also, when handing back a test, just give them the mark only and save the grade for after you've gone through it. That way, they'll be far more concerned with improvement than they would be otherwise.

When kids are off target

To be absolutely direct, a pupil off target leads to a cross-examination of their teacher and extra work for both. The process can be daunting, particularly for new teachers, but if you know what to expect and how to react, you'll be just fine. Any time when you are asked to input data, some version of the following sequence of events will occur: input data, data checked by school leaders, underachievers identified, teacher is questioned over underachievers and has to put in some sort of intervention.

Whether it's a handful of pupils or half the class, the first principle is the same: proactivity. When you enter the data, 'underachieving' pupils will immediately be indicated by a change in the colour of the box, e.g. green for on target, yellow for slightly below target and red for collect your P45 and be gone by the end of the day. Jokes aside, your proactivity – or lack thereof – will play a huge role in how you're perceived. All you have to do, then, is the moment that you are aware, don't wait. Email whoever you need to and tell them about the intervention that you're going to put in place. Your school will most probably have some sort of proforma/guidance for the intervention itself, so there is no need to regurgitate this. The point here is that wherever possible, you follow it before they make you follow it. Please note also that the need for proactivity is not just about your school leaders' perceptions of you. Most teachers would agree that it is our duty to do our best for our pupils (without compromising our own wellbeing/mental health) irrespective of what SLT may or may not think of us.

When you're questioned about 'underachieving' pupils, remember that in pretty much every country in the world apart from the UK and the USA, pupil 'underachievement' is seen as the pupil's problem, and not the teacher's (I may be generalising slightly). With this in mind, then, while it is perfectly acceptable to say that Nisreen is lazy and Harry hates science, in the discussion you must focus your energy on what you *can* do and not on what the kids *aren't* doing. For example, saying, 'Harry's probably underachieving in science because he keeps telling me he hates it. I'm going to find a way to make lessons more relevant to daily life. I have the following suggestions…' is better than saying, 'Nisreen is so lazy it's unbelievable. Honestly, she pays no attention whatsoever and she never does her homework. It's her own fault if she fails.' You may well be right about Nisreen, but make sure that you follow it up with something that you're going to do *as well as* get her to do.

As well as not focusing entirely on the pupils' shortcomings, what you don't want to do is blame yourself either. Usually, 'underachievement' is not a shock to the teacher and you will very likely predict it and try to do something about it in advance. In post-data meetings, not only will you be asked why it happened and what you are going to do about it, but you will also be asked what you did to prevent it. In this respect, there is no limit to the questions that you could be asked. If you say that you rang Harry's parents once a fortnight, for example, they'll ask why you didn't ring once a week. If you say that you used an exam question every couple of lessons, they'll ask why you didn't use one every lesson. You get the idea. If you experience these types of pernickety questions, it is important that you remain firm. State confidently what you did to prevent 'underachievement' in the first place, but also be open to suggestions. The key thing here is balance: if you beat yourself up, you risk looking like a weak teacher who missed lots of opportunities. If you're reluctant to action further intervention, you look arrogant or unconcerned.

Intervention

Intervention is pretty much compulsory. What will make it effective or detrimental, however, is the attitude with which you carry it out. For the sake of ease, two types of pupil are going to be discussed: clever and lazy. It goes without saying that humans are more nuanced than this, but in any case, there're far more than two categories of child. Take what you can from what follows but also trust your professional judgement and be sensitive to the needs of individual pupils.

Firstly, don't assume that clever kids can't underachieve: the cleverer the kid, the higher their target, so they too may well be working below it. Because clever kids often have more pressure at home and take 'underachievement' more seriously, they can be somewhat prone to feeling upset, stigmatised or anxious about 'underachieving'. Clever kids, then, are more likely to respond to intervention when you present it as 'support' rather than as a solution to some failure on their part. For example, say, 'I just want to give you some extra help so that you can do that little bit better and get the grade you deserve,' more often than you say, 'You need to try harder.'

With lazy kids, be absolutely direct: tell them off. Give them detentions. Keep ringing home. Tell them what will happen if they become lazy adults. Tell them that the worst feeling in life is regret. It is fine to use the stick more than the carrot in the early stages of intervention with lazy kids, as they often need to hear some home truths. By not giving them a proverbial kick up the backside, you'd be doing them a disservice. Once you're satisfied that they are making a sustained effort, *then* use the rewards/praise strategies described in Chapter 9.

Where you are unsure or suspect that there may be more complex or potentially upsetting reasons for a child's 'underachievement', default to the strategies in the final section below.

When target grades are too high

As mentioned earlier, the general perception of target grades is that they could better be described as 'aspirational' – not as 'expected' – and, for this reason, they are often perceived by teachers as being too high. This section is not about high target grades generally; it is about high target grades *specifically*. When the reconciliation between a child's ability and their target grade is slow and painful for the teacher, the target is *far* too high.

Luckily, while the above doesn't happen too often, it happens often enough for you to need to be aware of what to do when it does. The reasons why it may happen are beyond the scope of this book and, in any case, you can't do anything about them. So here's what to do.

The good thing is that, due to their very nature, a ridiculously high target sticks out like a sore thumb and therefore doesn't require much effort to spot. If it does, then you're probably wrong. No big deal. Where you are pretty sure, though, all you need to do is report it as soon as you are certain (it may take a couple of assessments). No need to make a big song and dance; just make sure that you send an email or mention it in a progress meeting or whatever. The reason for this is that it only takes one such pupil to supremely ruin the overall progress of your class. For example, if Fred is targeted a grade 8 and achieves a grade 3, it doesn't take a maths teacher to realise that he is five grades off his target. In terms of the whole class, then, Fred missing his target by five grades is the same as five pupils missing their target by one grade. The latter happens all the time, so you can see the damage done to your class's progress when you combine these two. Literally one pupil can make it look like the entire class is underperforming. As a general rule, then, if you can avoid looking like a shit teacher, well then, avoid looking like a shit teacher. (This is particularly important with respect to performance management – see Chapter 5.) Unfortunately, reporting it is the most that you can do: you'd probably have better luck picking up glue sticks with your butt-cheeks than you would getting a target grade lowered. The fact that you reported it, however, will at least work in your favour if it comes to answering some difficult questions.

When such pupils are 'underachieving', you should manage it in the same way described in the previous section but with one condition: the intervention itself should be done cautiously. There is a good chance that this isn't the first time that Fred has been told he's 'underachieving'. In fact, it's very probable that Fred is 'underachieving' in many other subjects and has been told that he's 'underachieving' for a long time – possibly years. A sure-fire way of making Fred hate you as well as disengage with the learning altogether is by making him feel stupid. Obviously, no teacher would consciously do this, but understand that if you keep on emphasising how many grades off target a child is, they will draw their own conclusions about themselves. Instead, focus on the concepts and not on the grade. Make sure that the child is aware that it's improvement (not achievement) that you want to see, and encourage and – more importantly this time – reward good effort and celebrate small gains. Unfortunately, given the constant badgering that such pupils are likely to have endured, you have to be prepared to deal with their reluctance and resentment. If this is the case, castigating Fred or giving him a detention won't do anything other than piss him off. Instead, make a greater effort to build a positive relationship with him using the strategies discussed in Chapter 10. As teachers, we want neither to pussyfoot around nor adversely affect our pupils' mental health. It may necessitate some trial and error on your part, but remember, you can simultaneously be mindful and maintain high standards. (These strategies are also applicable to other 'underachieving' pupils – particularly if you think that they feel judged by the system – irrespective of how high their target grade is.)

Summary

- Pupils (and therefore teachers) are constantly being assessed. This can be a very real source of stress, not only for teachers but for pupils too.
- You will regularly be asked to enter current grades, which is problematic because they can be confusing to derive and the system demands that pupils show linear progress.
- As well as being arbitrarily ascribed, target grades are often perceived to be too high. In addition, target grades are part of the reason for constant teacher intervention, which can also be a source of stress for teachers and pupils alike. Target grades can demoralise pupils as well as limit their success.
- Make your pupils aware of their target grade, but teach them that their ultimate target is to do their best.
- Absorb the pressure: don't let pupils know that you're stressed about their 'underachievement'. By doing so, you risk undermining yourself and some pupils will deflect the pressure back on you.
- If you feel that target grades limit your pupils' achievement, avoid mentioning grades until you are satisfied that pupils have made a substantial effort to improve their knowledge/skills.
- Where pupils are off target, proactivity is key. Make sure that you have intervention strategies in place and focus on what you can do and not what the kids aren't doing.
- When carrying out intervention, different approaches work better with different pupils. 'Clever' pupils prefer 'support', whereas a firmer approach is needed with 'lazy' pupils. Even if a target grade is ridiculously high, it will never be lowered; exercise much caution when carrying out intervention with unreasonably high target grades.

Chapter 7
How to survive against the Ofsted odds

No doubt you will have heard about the perils of an impending Ofsted inspection. You will have heard about the large numbers of teachers who've outright left the profession citing pressures from Ofsted as their sole reason. When you were a pupil, you may well have even chuckled while you witnessed an anxiety-ridden teacher walking frantically around the class, begging you not to misbehave if someone came in.

Allow me to be absolutely direct: the fear of Ofsted is not an irrational one. The hoop-jumping, the confusing guidelines and the tyrannical talk are all very real. While Ofsted is at present an unavoidable problem in the education system (your school WILL be inspected), as individual teachers there is much that we can do to better manage this and not allow that aspect of the system to kill our love for the profession. This chapter will tell you about some of the specific problems of – or related to – Ofsted and you will also learn some tips to keep you sane and successful during this potentially difficult time.

The problems with Ofsted

Perception

Ofsted claims to be an organisation that exists for the honourable purpose of supporting – and therefore improving – schools. However, nowhere has a mismatch between intent and perception ever been more apparent: teachers' perceptions of Ofsted are in direct opposition to the nobility of what Ofsted claims to be its intention. By anyone working in a school, Ofsted is perceived as a heavily punitive organisation whose primary aim is to measure and punish – and not develop – schools.

Surely teachers are being cynical, right? Wrong. One only has to turn one's attention to some of the statements made by former Ofsted Chief Inspector Sir Michael Wilshaw, who once told headteachers to 'stop moaning', take stress 'on the chin' and (you'll love this) 'If anyone says to you that *staff morale* is at an *all-time low*, you know you are doing something right.' He also told teachers to stop complaining that their job is stressful and said that teachers should 'roll up their sleeves and get on with their work'. Fills you with joy, doesn't it? What a good way to improve the wellbeing of one of the most stressed occupations in the country!

Hoop-jumping

The week after an inspection, no teacher has ever said, 'I feel like my teaching has improved so much because of Ofsted.' Rather, as well as feeling monumentally fatigued, teachers feel the exact opposite: 'What was the point of all that?!' you'll no doubt hear or have heard teachers say. The problem is that Ofsted inspections are a hoop-jumping exercise; they are something we have to do to prove our worth rather than something from which we can benefit. It may be argued that every large company has to hoop-jump to a certain extent from time to time, so why should schools be treated any differently? The problem is that in a school setting, it's the pupils that ultimately suffer under such a system. In other words, jumping through hoops ends up taking precedence over the holistic development of the child. All too often, at schools that are due an Ofsted inspection in a given academic year, all the staff briefings, meetings and INSETs will begin with some version of the sentence: 'When Ofsted come in they will want to see…' I even recall attending a day course titled 'When the door handle turns', which literally told teachers exactly what to do if an inspector came into their lesson. People outside the profession may argue that if we are following Ofsted guidelines then, ultimately, we *are* doing what's best for the children, but this simply is not the case. Because of Ofsted, whatever schools do for their pupils has to be done in a way that *enables its inspection*, and that is where a teacher's time and energy is, well, wasted. Why else would fully qualified, experienced teachers be forced to attend courses telling them exactly what to do when some clipboard wanker walks in? The time could far better be spent on no end of other things that could positively impact the pupils.

Perpetual confusion

The way it works is that Ofsted publishes its requirements and then headteachers meet up in some fancy-pants five-star hotel to discuss the most effective methods that their teachers could employ to make sure that all demands are met – ensuring, of course, that these would be easily visible to an inspector. Superficially, this seems perfectly reasonable but, in reality, it is anything but. A couple of examples come to mind.

Not too long ago, teachers who taught using what is commonly referred to as 'chalk and talk' or 'teaching from the front' were criticised by school leaders who had 'somehow' got the idea that a lesson being 'teacher-led' was a bad thing. Unless there were groups of kids working collaboratively and giving whole-class instruction was minimal, the teacher would likely have been told that they required improvement. In addition to this, triple-marking became the feedback of choice for the bulk of schools, which meant that teachers spent many hours a week marking work, commenting on the work and then going back to the work to mark pupils' responses to teachers' comments. Not so surprisingly, there were major shortages, as teachers were leaving the profession at alarming rates during this period.

Around two or three years later (it is difficult to pinpoint exactly when, as schools would not have taken on the above initiatives simultaneously), Ofsted published a 'myths' document, which stated two important points that would blow the perceived necessity and effectivity of the aforementioned practices right out the water. It stated firstly that 'Ofsted doesn't prescribe any particular teaching style' and secondly that 'Ofsted does not expect to see any specific frequency, type or volume of marking and feedback; these are for the school to decide through its assessment policy.' In other words, school leaders had been imposing complicated and time-consuming restrictions on teachers when they did not have to.

Or did they? A myth (to me at least) is something that never really happened. For Ofsted to essentially argue that school leaders never actually *had* to impose such practices on their staff is more or less saying that the majority of headteachers misunderstood Ofsted's guidance. Surely that's a bit far-fetched? I suspect that the likely scenario is that headteachers understood the guidance just fine and followed it correctly, but Ofsted later realised that their guidance was bullshit (triple-marking doesn't work and teaching from the front can work very well) and so later decided to change it. The myth thing, in this respect, was most probably a smokescreen. In any case, Ofsted's guidance is – and always has been – a permanent source of confusion.

A tragic comedy

As a key determinant of a school's Ofsted grade is based on data, i.e. exam results, naturally school leaders do whatever is necessary to ensure that every child reaches their full potential in this area. To enable this, then, in secondary schools a couple of trends became painfully common. Firstly, there was a trend of early exam entry. In certain subjects, pupils were forced (yes, forced) to do the GCSE exam in Year 10, thereby 'banking' a GCSE grade (which, by the way, was often far lower than what they would have achieved had they done the same exam in Year 11) and using the extra time in Year 11 to ensure decent grades in other subjects that were essential for the school's overall performance. Secondly, multiple resits became excruciatingly normal: it was not uncommon to sit a maths GCSE paper in Year 9, Year 10, and then again in Year 11. Meanwhile, in primary schools, it is still common for disproportionate amounts of teaching time to be allocated to English and maths – often at the cost of other subjects, particularly the arts – in order for schools to ensure high grades in the SATs.

No school leader in their right mind would *voluntarily* make the aforementioned changes – at least not in the traditional sense of the word. It goes without saying, then, that these were done for the sole purpose of ensuring a good Ofsted grade.

So, after realising schools' craftiness (*forced* craftiness is probably a better way to describe it), Ofsted finally caught on and published documents condemning pretty much all of the above. Primary schools were told not to narrow their curriculum in Year 6 and secondary schools were told that multiple resits were no longer acceptable. In other words, Ofsted inadvertently created problems by making judgements based disproportionately on exam results, and then condemned schools for having those problems – a tragic comedy if ever there was one.

Just a formality

It is a common belief among teachers and school leaders that Ofsted's judgement on a school is made well before the inspection even begins. Whether it's due to the bulk of the decision being based on a school's exam results (at least, this was the case before recent changes to the Ofsted framework) or because Ofsted has some hidden plan for a particular school in a particular area, Ofsted is just not perceived as trustworthy. Again, this is not an irrational belief. Firstly, the fact that so many in education are of this opinion suggests that Ofsted, at the very least, has some explaining to do. Secondly, the lack of professional trust at many schools is a direct result of Ofsted's very own policies. In other words, Ofsted doesn't trust teachers so why should teachers trust them? I mean, if you catch your partner looking through your phone, do you agree that it's probably *them* who's cheating on you? Those who don't trust can't be trusted.

SLT's frenzy

As an Ofsted inspection – and indeed the lead-up to it – can be a very stressful time for school leaders, it has the potential to bring out, well, the worst in them. In the year when an inspection is due, for example, it is not uncommon for SLTs to seemingly try to become even stricter than Ofsted itself. Criteria for lesson observations suddenly become more stringent, and 'good' lessons, while remaining good, are treated *as if* they 'require improvement' because 'we want to be outstanding, not good!'. In addition to this, the frequency and duration of learning walks may also increase, and book scrutinies may take place with little or no notice (if they don't already). While all of this may be bad, it still retains a degree of ethicality. On occasion, however, SLTs may do things that even they may well lose sleep over in years to come – like the school that 'rewarded' its naughty pupils when their behaviour 'improved' by taking them to Alton Towers on the day of the inspection, or the school that paid unruly pupils £100 to stay at home. If that wasn't bad enough, schools have even been known to sign 'weak' teachers off work before an inspection. In addition, the practice of 'off-rolling' – which has gone on for more than a decade – has only in recent years been noticed and opposed by Ofsted. (Yet another example of Ofsted creating a problem for schools and then condemning schools for having that very problem.)

It may be argued that this is the fault of school leaders for mismanaging Ofsted's demands, but the two are so closely intertwined that one cannot be mentioned without the other. In any case, this is one of the reasons why Ofsted is the cause for the demoralisation of many a teacher.

How to survive an Ofsted inspection

The Ofsted inspection framework has recently undergone a massive overhaul and so is different to what experienced teachers are used to. In any case, the purpose of this section is not to repeat what can easily be found in an internet search; rather, here we will discuss some generic, timeless strategies that a teacher can employ to make the process more bearable and ensure positive outcomes for both the teacher and their school.

Ignorance is not bliss

There are some aspects of Ofsted that you, as an individual teacher, can do absolutely nothing about. Their constant denigration of teachers, their confusing guidelines and the problems that erupt from following those guidelines are not things that are under our control. As mentioned earlier, there has been an overhaul in the Ofsted framework recently, but like anyone else who's been teaching for a substantial period of time, I too am certain that the aforementioned problems will not disappear; they will just be repackaged and redelivered via different distribution channels.

In spite of this, simply being aware of the issues is helpful in and of itself. Despite convention telling us otherwise, ignorance, in this respect, is far from bliss. The reasons why so many teachers leave the profession so early in their career can be boiled down to one: they were not fully aware of what they were in for. By knowing a thing or two about Ofsted before you ever experience them, you can begin to manage your thoughts and emotions beforehand, thereby knocking a huge chunk off the emotional labour that will no doubt accompany your early encounters with Ofsted. Try your best not to get bogged down, however, and spending hours reading up on them is pointless. Tell yourself, 'Yes, Ofsted is going to piss me off from time to time, but I'm going to focus on the things that I can do to make the inspection process – the part that affects me directly – far more bearable so that I can remain a happy teacher.'

What to expect

If your school is due an inspection, your headteacher will normally make a huge deal out of it at the start of the academic year, most probably during the two excruciatingly boring INSET days in early September. In fact, the way in which the inspection is conveyed to staff by SLT can be very telling: bad school leaders will keep going on about it and start banging heads, whereas good school leaders will not make it the be-all and end-all. For example, one headteacher, at the start of the year, said, 'We *do* have Ofsted in this year, and this is the last time I will mention it.' (It wasn't mentioned again until the day before the inspection, and the school was graded 'outstanding'.)

At some point during that year, then, all staff will receive an email instructing them to go to the hall after school for a quick meeting – you'll immediately know why. Your SLT will then talk you through the pending process, i.e. the number of inspectors, meetings, learning walks, observations, pupil voice interviews, etc. Either the same day or the next, more meetings will take place within departments, and middle leaders will clarify the headteacher's instructions as well as give subject- or department-specific guidance.

Get your shit ready

Lesson observations and learning walks are still – and probably always will be – part of an Ofsted inspection. There have, however, been some changes to the requirements thereof. In short, Ofsted no longer insists on seeing written lesson plans from teachers, but headteachers often leave the decision to the teacher. In other words, your headteacher may say something to the effect of, 'Ofsted doesn't insist on written lesson plans, but we suggest that you do provide them.'

My advice is to get your shit ready *whether you are asked to or not*. This includes lesson plans, class data, seating plans and whatever else you can think of. Now before you accuse me of increasing your workload and make a dartboard with a picture of my face on it, hear me out, because there are two important reasons why preparing lesson plans, etc. is highly recommended.

Firstly, as there is always a chance that a lesson will not go the way in which you intend it, a lesson plan can serve as a potential backdrop during the feedback if ever you have to explain that you did everything in your power to make sure it didn't go tits up. Any inspector worth their salt would at least be willing to listen to a teacher's explanation, so by not having your shit ready, you risk giving the impression that your lesson went badly because you didn't plan it properly. In essence, treat an Ofsted observation exactly as you would any formal observation, irrespective of the official paperwork requirements.

Secondly, don't forget that it may not just be the inspector that observes you. You may (as I have during the majority of inspections I've experienced) be observed with the inspector *and* a member of SLT. (Oh, the joy. God knows what I've done to walk around with a target on my head, but hey ho.) If this is the case, you need to remember that there is a good chance that the inspector is not only observing you but they are also observing SLT's ability to observe your teaching accurately. For that reason, some SLT will no doubt have a need to appear 'stricter' in their judgement. The last thing you want to do, then, is to annoy them with your ill-preparedness as soon as they walk into your room. Unless it's been decided otherwise and agreed upon whole school-wide via union reps, get your shit ready.

Behaviour

One of the most annoying things about Ofsted is that they cramp your style. You'll try your absolute hardest to continue teaching as normal but you'll keep looking at the door, and if you hear so much as a footstep in the corridor, your heart will start pounding, your mouth will turn dry and your tongue will feel like sandpaper. For the love of God, don't forget your water bottle on the day of the inspection! We all hate inspectors but the last thing you want is for them to write 'teachers need to improve halitosis' in the feedback box.

One of the major sources of teachers' – particularly new teachers' – anxiety during an Ofsted inspection is pupil behaviour. This is a perfectly reasonable concern, as the feeling of losing control of your class is humiliating enough in itself, let alone when somebody's watching. You'll be glad to know, however, that more often than not, our minds tend to exaggerate this fear, and in any case, there are preventative measures that you can take.

Firstly, you'll be surprised at how much even your 'naughty' kids have got your back during an inspection. You see, for most misbehaving pupils, their constant disrupting of your lesson is actually *not* motivated by their dislike of you. Don't get me wrong, there *are* pupils who hate our guts, but when push comes to shove, most don't hate us enough to actively screw us over. Whether it's because they suddenly become sympathetic to an apparently stressed teacher or because school leaders read them the riot act beforehand, or because an external 'enemy' subconsciously causes everyone to stick together, you can take comfort in knowing that most pupils will automatically behave better during an Ofsted inspection in most instances.

Most instances. So, there is a chance that there will be some pupils who will act maliciously in *some* instances. As you probably know who they are likely to be, the key thing is to be proactive *before* the inspection starts. Have a word with pastoral leaders or even speak to the pupil(s) directly. Use your professional judgement to do whatever you deem necessary, but be careful: if you give the pupil the impression that you're *expecting* them to ruin your lesson, guess what they'll be more likely to do?

On that note, do not allow your anxiety to make you do something that you wouldn't do otherwise. What I'm referring to here is that, in extreme cases, a desperate teacher anticipating poor behaviour may remove a pupil from their classroom prior to the start of the inspection. No matter how much you worry, never circumvent your school's behaviour policy. Even if it's ineffective, it has to be followed, and rarely is it the case that you can remove a pupil in advance of a lesson without consulting your line managers.

During inspections, Ofsted may do a 'pupil trail' and it may just be the case that they follow the one pupil you decided to put in your bestie's room before your lesson started. As moralising over the removal of a pupil in advance of poor behaviour is not the purpose of this chapter, I will only say that any teacher who does this will be hauled over the coals and it will most probably do lasting damage to their professional reputation. Don't do it.

Instead, take solace in knowing that Ofsted is actually *not* expecting perfect behaviour; rather, inspectors are looking for behaviour policies to be employed consistently. If a large number of teachers are struggling, then guess what? You are not the problem! Bad behaviour does not necessarily destroy a lesson in the eyes of Ofsted anyway. You'd never believe it, but you can be given good feedback even if a fight breaks out in your lesson, providing, of course, that you follow school policy and it works. It's not common (as most kids don't wait until Ofsted to batter each other), but the fact that there's a good chance that you'll be OK says a lot. If the worst happens, just follow your school behaviour policy to a T and it'll be fine or better. (There was that one school where the kids pelted Ofsted inspectors with food and staff went on strike over poor behaviour not long after, but that won't happen. You'll be fine.)

An unfortunate consequence of an inspection is that while pupils may behave better, many tend to feel like *they* are on the spot and so tend to 'freeze up'. You may find that pupils volunteer answers to questions a lot less, give minimal answers when probed or generally seem a bit zombie-like. If this happens, try not to let it stress you out, as your stress will cause the kids stress and the kids' stress will cause you stress and… you get the idea. Instead – and for heaven's sake don't freeze up yourself – use your voice to engage and enthuse, even if it sounds a bit fake. In my books, the faker the better (in this respect), as you'll have a good laugh when the class make fun of you as soon as the inspector leaves.

It can be fun

Did you know that Ofsted inspectors are actually forbidden from entering a school staffroom? For their sake, this is probably a good thing, as there's something about the Ofsted cocktail of anxiety, sleep deprivation, adrenaline and caffeine that makes teachers a bit… loopy… in a good way… often at the expense of the inspectors. From the moment at which they introduce themselves in the hall on the morning of the inspection, the jokes begin. The way they're dressed, the way they look, in the staffroom everything about them is fair game. I remember one teacher who could make up an entire backstory about an inspector within seconds of meeting them: 'He looks like he went through a tough divorce last year but he's just starting to pick up – you know – doing the parkrun again, bought himself some new suits, had his teeth whitened, that kind of thing. He really needs to do something about that tie, though.' I recall being gobsmacked on the morning of an inspection when, from the staffroom window, we saw an inspector vacate a huge, expensive, shiny car, which I'm sure even had tinted windows. You'd think that someone who works for one of the highest levels of the government would probably not try to imitate a rap star! I still remember the jokes that ensued: 'Do you think she sells drugs on the side?' Also, on this note, it's worth being aware that despite the clipboard wanker perception, it is bizarrely *not* uncommon for teachers to find that observations by Ofsted are more bearable and the feedback far less pernickety than it is with their very own senior leaders. Ofsted *as an organisation* has a lot to answer for, but don't assume that every individual inspector is trying to catch you out.

There's something about this external 'enemy' that brings teachers together. As well as good humour, the process is made much more bearable through staff camaraderie, which goes up tenfold. During an inspection, you will find staff constantly checking up on each other, and at some schools senior leaders may even show up at your room with some edible treat. Your headteacher's motivational speech the day before will also get you into fight mode and, on some level, you may even look forward to the inspection. Bizarre, eh?

In short, yes, it's a hoop, but *how* you jump through that hoop is entirely your decision. Make it fun.

Some final tips…

Where Ofsted is concerned, there are some things that you can set your watch to. Take heed of the following tips:

- You know that one annoying teacher who thinks they know everything? Ignore them. Ofsted is not a band on tour. Just because the school around the corner got hit last week, it doesn't mean that Ofsted is 'in the area' and you're next. Stop the predictions.
- The day before the inspection, school will be open late. If feasible, use that distraction-free time to get your planning done at school. Do some collaborative planning if it doesn't cramp your style. If it does, be willing to share resources and otherwise support colleagues nonetheless.
- Print your lesson plans and resources the night before. Don't print in the morning – the printer will run out of toner and the

photocopier will be jammed. You won't be able to find IT support because they will be replacing toners and unjamming photocopiers all over school from 8.00 am.

- Make sure that everything works: if your laptop starts doing that thing where it launches 568 updates that remain only 42 per cent complete halfway through period one, you're going to have a big problem.

- Don't let your guard down: stay prepared, even if the head says that observations are *likely* to be finished by 2.00 pm. It's unlikely, but you can be observed/learning-walked more than once.

- Make sure that exercise books for the lessons you're teaching that day are marked. Don't worry if you missed one. Don't miss several. Hide any unmarked books for other classes/subjects. (Or at least don't leave them where it's easy for some conniving inspector to sneak a peak at them.)

- Chill with the caffeine. It'll make you jittery and wee loads. It's OK to get less sleep as a one-off but make sure that you get a decent amount at least.

- Make sure that your room is tidy and displays are neat. Do not prioritise these unless specifically told to do so.

- If you teach in more than one room, check the rooms before you leave on the day of the announcement, just in case someone's changed the layout or the projector's remote has been sold online.

- Have a chat with the inspector(s) if they seem human. If they don't reciprocate conversation, stop talking. If they disrupt your lesson by talking to the kids while you're teaching, don't shout at them or the kids.

- It's only two days. They'll be gone soon enough.

Summary

- The fear of Ofsted is not an irrational one and Ofsted is fully responsible for teachers' negative perception of the organisation.
- Hoop-jumping is inevitable in any organisation. But in schools it is detrimental to teaching and learning because it takes valuable time and energy away from the pupils.
- Ofsted's guidelines have always been a perpetual source of confusion for teachers and school leaders alike.
- In order to meet Ofsted's criteria for success, schools were forced to narrow the curriculum in Year 6 and enter pupils for multiple resits from Year 9 onwards. Ofsted then condemned schools for these practices. A tragic comedy if ever there was one.
- Because inspection outcomes are based a lot on exam results, a commonly held belief by teachers is that Ofsted's decision is made before the inspectors even enter the building.
- Some SLTs get into a frenzy and start mismanaging their staff during an Ofsted year. Others take it in their stride.
- Don't overfocus your attention on Ofsted. Be aware of the issues but don't get bogged down.
- If Ofsted is due, you will be told at the start of the year in September. Then randomly one day, all staff will be called into the hall and told that Ofsted is arriving tomorrow.
- During an inspection, plan all of your lessons the way in which you would an observed lesson. Write a lesson plan even if your headteacher doesn't insist on it.
- Most pupils will behave better if an inspector enters the room. If you are worried about misbehaving pupils sabotaging your lesson, speak to pastoral leaders in advance of the inspection.
- Believe it or not, Ofsted inspections can be fun! Embrace them.

Chapter 8
How to manage behaviour policies

Anyone who did even the slightest bit of research prior to beginning their teacher training is fully aware that at many schools, rarely do pupils have a natural sense of discipline. Rather, it is down to the teacher to manage pupil behaviour. In this chapter, then, there is no need to go through the details of the types of behaviour to expect. What is not told or taught, however, are the details of how behaviour is managed on a *whole-school level* and the problems that can arise from this – and not just from the poor behaviour itself. In other words, as a trainee, it won't take you long to discover the perils of low-level disruption, but as an NQT, you may be blindsided upon receipt of an email reprimanding you for setting too many detentions or unfairly sending pupils out of the room.

Pupil behaviour and how to manage it is an area of permanent contention in the edusphere. From zero-tolerance behaviour policies to sanction-free restorative approaches and everything in between, opinions are often passionate and discussions heated. Here we will briefly discuss the different behaviour management policies that you might come across and, more importantly, you will learn how best to respond to their implications on you as the teacher.

Behaviour management policies

Most schools manage behaviour via what is commonly referred to as a 'consequence system'. Typically, the teacher gives a pupil three distinct warnings for each misbehaviour, after which a sanction is issued. If poor behaviour persists, the severity of the sanction increases. For example, the first sanction may be a 30-minute detention, the next a 60-minute, and then, finally, removal from the room, followed by isolation the next day. Schools that run this effectively have a centralised system for detentions, i.e. they are at the same time and place and are overseen by a school leader, and they require minimal administration – often just a tick-box slip and text messages are automatically sent home to parents. Also, the teacher is under no obligation to be present at the detention, and if a pupil decides to miss a detention, it is followed up by a school leader – not the teacher. The consequence system is effective at most schools for most pupils, and in those where it isn't, it's usually due to teacher inconsistency or unsupportive school leaders, and not because of an inherent flaw in the system.

Some schools, many of which are small 'free' schools, adopt a 'zero-tolerance' approach to behaviour management. The smallest infraction could lead to a pupil being removed from a lesson: not having a pen could get a child sent home and corridors must be walked through in silence. While such an approach may seem extreme, zero-tolerance approaches *are* effective (in specific microcosms at least) and any problems that arise are usually due to parental complaints of over-punishment and not from kids running riot due to under-punishment.

An increasing number of schools have adopted what could be considered the exact opposite of zero-tolerance: they have got rid of sanctions completely and rely on an entirely restorative approach. In essence, when a pupil misbehaves, the teacher is required to have a 'restorative conversation' with the child, which aims to better understand their personal circumstances and guide them towards good behaviour in future. Detentions disappear and removing a pupil from the classroom – even if they are making learning impossible for the rest of the class – is very difficult, and even if it happens, it is only until they've 'calmed down' and had a chance to 'reflect on their behaviour'. Unlike the previous approaches, this one is inherently flawed for two reasons: firstly, because it's rare to find a teacher who will tell you that behaviour at their school *didn't worsen* after adopting this approach, and secondly, because it is rooted in ideology and not reality.

It is not, however, the 'restorative' element of the approach that is the reason for its failure. Good teachers regularly chat to disruptive pupils in order to improve their behaviour, without any instruction from their SLTs whatsoever. It's the lack of – or absolute minimalisation of – sanction setting and enforcing that causes behaviour at such schools to deteriorate. Chris Keates, head of the NASUWT, spoke about this:

> 'What members are telling us is that in some schools, all that is happening is that the restorative conversation is seen as the sanction in itself,' Ms Keates told the *Daily Telegraph*. 'And then pupils are thinking, "Well, there aren't any sanctions here for what I do, all I've got to do is sit down and have a conversation with the teacher". And so it isn't a deterrent.'

It is not uncommon for teachers at such schools to report disruptive (and even violent) pupils who, when removed from the lesson, have a polite chat with the deputy head and return 30 minutes later to sit and smirk at the teacher.

As well as being ineffective, a restorative approach places a disproportionate amount of focus on the actions of teachers, so it is common for pupil misbehaviour to be considered the consequence of provocation from an adult. During a restorative conversation, for example, a teacher may well be coerced into admitting some 'wrongdoing' (which could be something as minor as adopting a stern tone), and both the child and teacher could be encouraged to apologise to each other. As well as justifiably feeling unsupported, teachers at these schools are often outright blamed for pupil misbehaviour, and relationships between teachers and SLT are at best discordant, and at worst hostile.

As mentioned earlier, the restorative approach is rooted in ideology and promoted by those who essentially consider punishment or sanctions to be inherently immoral. If the aim of school is to prepare children for the 'real world', then a restorative approach cannot be considered anything other than dangerous, as it bears no resemblance to it whatsoever.

The common problem

Irrespective of how your school chooses to manage behaviour, the problem with the education system is that it removes much of the responsibility thereof from the pupil and places it firmly on the teacher. Apart from in probably the very few 'zero-tolerance' schools, you can say with almost 100 per cent certainty that when a deputy head walks into a lesson and sees a kid misbehaving, the teacher is far more worried about the consequences than the pupil is. In other words, if a kid is turning around and whispering, etc. while you're teaching and a deputy head sees, what *you* did about it will often take precedence over holding the child to account. Unfortunately, an undercurrent of teacher-blaming is integral to the system (although it does vary from school to school). Lest you get the wrong end of the stick, it is not being suggested here that behaviour management is *not* the responsibility of the teacher. Most teachers consider this a part of their role, as common sense dictates that kids will be kids – when the cat is away, the mice will play, etc. The problem is the *extent to which* teachers are considered responsible *and not the pupils themselves.* The latter removes a child's sense of ownership over their behaviour and likely contributes to the removal of any natural sense of discipline that a child may possess.

Having a disproportionate amount of responsibility for behaviour management is one thing, but managing behaviour – even when using the given policies correctly – can be problematic no matter how much a school may show off its supportive systems. What they don't tell you is that if you *keep* using the aforementioned systems (detentions, SLT on-call, etc.), you will be seen as a weak teacher. This can be a shock to the system of some new teachers, who misperceive poor behaviour as something that can easily be passed up the hierarchy so that they can do their job in peace. The truth is that while a school may indeed have a robust and effective behaviour management system, school leaders are often overburdened with other demands, and so the less dependent you are on them, the stronger the teacher they will consider you to be. In short, the irony is that the education system does not fully allow for behaviour systems.

If you're an experienced teacher, it is very probable that you are well established and so may not consider the above to be a problem: you hardly use your school's behaviour system anyway because your kids know your name and your face, and their siblings and friends whom you taught years ago would have told them your expectations long before your first lesson with them. If, however, you're reading this as a trainee or NQT, it is important to realise that while it *is* acceptable to use the system more than an experienced teacher, you must not become reliant upon it. Rather, you should use your God-given tools as well as the guidance in the next section to manage behaviour *before* you start setting sanctions.

Ideally, what you want is for your classroom management to be so good that kids and school leaders are shocked when you use the system.

What to do before you set a detention

Behaviour management is that extra bit more personal than the rest of teaching, so a teacher can only ever tell you what has worked for them and what they have seen work for others. What works for you, however, may be entirely different and that's perfectly fine! In that spirit, then, it is advisable to follow behaviour management strategies that resonate rather than robotically follow a prescriptive set of rules. If you read a part of this section and nod along thinking, 'Oh my God, that is so true!', then follow it. If you're unsure and think to yourself, 'That won't work for me', it is entirely acceptable to rule it out after some consideration. Remember, if you're a new teacher, you likely haven't fully developed your style yet, so the more strategies that you're exposed to, the greater the list to choose from.

To manage your classroom without using your school's behaviour system, take what you can from the tips that follow.

Your teacher voice

A big behaviour management no-no is a monotonous teacher voice. Kids are more responsive and better behaved when a teacher's tone is appropriately 'animated'. What this means is that not only is it a good idea to change your tone depending on what you're saying, but it also helps to say particular things using particular syntaxes. For example, if you want your kids to get excited about the cells rap that it took you two hours to search for, then your tone must reflect this excitement. If you're explaining some complicated concept, you should speak in short sentences and your tone should indicate that, while you are sympathetic to the kids' struggles, you want them to remain alert. In other words, there should be a marked difference between the way in which you say, 'Let's listen to the cells rap!' and 'Right. Listen carefully. Renewable means that it WILL NOT run out.'

In addition to having an incidental impact on pupil behaviour in your class, the tone and volume of your voice is all the more important when managing behaviour directly, particularly if the aim is to avoid setting a sanction. Teachers with strong classroom management are often good at switching from very friendly to very stern if it is dictated by the situation. For example, Mr Bloggs is normally polite, approachable and even casual when he speaks to his pupils. Every now and again, however, the class talk too much and don't respond to Mr Bloggs' normal tone when he asks them to quieten down. In the event of this, Mr Bloggs does not hesitate to throw his voice, show a little bit of anger and reassert his authority. As his tone is polite and respectful the rest of the time, the kids realise that they've genuinely done something to piss him off and so feel a bit guilty and go quiet. Of course, this is also because he has a good relationship with them – more about this in Chapter 10 – but the two are inseparable.

It is worth noting here that shouting is generally considered bad practice in schools (as it indicates a lack of control), but kids and school leaders know full well the difference between a teacher who is raising their voice and a teacher who has lost their shit. In Mr Bloggs' case, it's theatrical: he knows exactly what he's doing. While switching tones from friendly to stern is also effective on individual pupils, shouting at individual pupils is best avoided as it is either ineffective or counterproductive. Save it for when the whole class is doing your head in.

For a switch in tone to be effective, the difference has to be distinct – just like when you're teaching – but in this case it should only be used rarely, as overuse will lessen its impact. Make sure, then, that you build up to it; if your normal tone doesn't work twice, make the switch. In addition, the 'nicer' your normal tone, the greater the impact of your sternness. If your natural speech is not particularly animated and you lean more towards a monotone, it just means that you have to practise in the mirror a few times. Failing that, your favourite childhood teachers probably had a variety of 'go to' tones and phrases, so just imitate them!

In order for your tone to be effective, you have to believe in your words. One of the reasons why it may take some time (and this is perfectly normal) for the above to be effective for a new teacher is that there is an inherent degree of uncertainty possessed by new teachers. Ironically, the anxiety is counterproductive: worrying about the kids not taking you seriously makes them less likely to take you seriously. If, however, you *genuinely* believe in your words, your confidence will radiate and the kids – who ultimately *do* acknowledge your authority – will believe in them as much as you do. Remember that any belief we have in our minds is conveyed by our nervous systems: the stranger on the bus knows that you feel uncomfortable sitting near him; the deputy head knows that you care what she thinks of you; and Carol in reception knows that you're annoyed because she lost your wage-slip for the third time. If you change your belief, your vibe will follow and you won't be running around school chasing kids who didn't turn up to your detention.

Your teacher space

When pupils enter your room, they have to know that they are entering *your* space. *Your* territory. Yours – not theirs. In the minds of the kids, you, your teaching, your rules and your room are different shades of the same thing, so making your mark in all areas will help to ensure good behaviour.

Teachers with strong classroom management increase both their classroom presence and ownership simply by moving around the room *while teaching*. It goes without saying that every teacher circulates when checking kids' work, etc., but while giving an explanation, many new teachers tend to hover near the front and potentially risk lessening their control over the class. When your kids are silent, try using your clicker to change slides from the back of the room or do some targeted questioning from the middle, turning around as and when necessary. If walking while teaching, take slow and deliberate steps and occupy the same space for a good few seconds before walking to the next. If you have some low-level disruptors in the room, stand next to their seat while speaking and watch how quiet they get without you even having to tell them. As getting the attention of the class when you're at the front is to be expected, speaking from less conventional places gives your authority that extra boost. Do be careful, however, as if the class is not silent when you're at the front of the room, they will not be silent when you're at the back. Establish yourself from the front, and then do the above to make sure that you hold the fort.

One final point on this (which I know will cause some teachers to steal my glue sticks and hide my laptop charger) is that, as difficult as it can be, you must keep your room tidy. A cluttered desk will make you appear disorganised in the eyes of the pupils, who will, as a consequence, have less respect for your boundaries.

Your teacher body language

Just like your voice and your space, your body language can communicate a lot to your pupils. Walking with your shoulders back and your back straight indicates confidence, so now is a good time to follow the advice that you didn't when you were a teen.

Whether you just realised you left your starter activity at the photocopier or you're late to your lesson, try your best never to appear flustered. Often, kids take advantage of new teachers because, somehow, they just know that they're new. By appearing flustered you are practically *telling* them that you're new and that they should misbehave and then laugh while you get even more flustered at their poor behaviour.

In front of pupils, always try to appear unaffected by anything unwanted. While your teacher voice and body language will normally work in conjunction with one another, try to use the latter before the former when dealing with misbehaviours. For example, instead of saying, 'Er… can we quieten down please!', just say, 'Er' and then give the kids your teacher stare – which, by the way, you should practise in the mirror. By saying less, the message kids get is that the fact that you are physically there is enough of a reason for them to follow your rules. Think about it: when the head walks into your lesson, do they even have to say anything before you suddenly become self-conscious? Apply the same reasoning to your classes by whole-heartedly believing in your presence.

Prioritising behaviour

Another way to reduce the amount of sanctions you issue is by, wait for it… not issuing them. Obvious statements aside, new teachers are often so bombarded with behaviour workshops that emphasise the importance of whole-school consistency that they end up unable to see the wood for the trees. The purpose of any behaviour policy is ultimately to ensure that children are safe and that learning can take place as effectively as possible, so as a teacher, you should prioritise the management of any behaviour that adversely affects either of those.

The greatest destruction of lessons is actually not caused by the rude, aggressive or antisocial kids that you always hear about on the news. Rather, it is caused by the constant interruption from perfectly 'normal' kids who, for whatever reason, will not shut up! The moment that you open your mouth, they'll open theirs. When you ask for a task to be done in silence, they'll comply for a total of 20 seconds before you have to tell them off again. Despite it not sounding like a particularly big deal, excessive low-level disruption is enough to render a lesson unsatisfactory. It is important, then, that you choose your battles wisely. If, for example, you've got six kids in your class who won't stay quiet when asked and another six who don't do their homework, go to town on the first six and (unless your school's behaviour policy *absolutely* insists otherwise) give the others multiple chances before you sanction them. In short, it is more effective to be strict in areas that affect the learning in the lesson, as being strict in all areas at the same time will lead to an overuse of the behaviour system, draining your time and energy in the process.

Once, a kid made fun of my baldness simply by asking, 'Sir, do bald people use shampoo?' I laughed, the class laughed, but the moment that I clapped my hands and said, 'Right. Enough,' they were back on task in silence because they knew that I couldn't care less about the bald thing: I had strict rules on talking that I made clear at the start of the year, and because I'm a teacher who *can* have a laugh, they chose not to see my 'bad' side. Of course, you are under no obligation to allow kids to make fun of your hair – or lack thereof – but if it doesn't affect the learning in your lesson, putting it lower on your to-do list will save you a headache.

Nip it in the bud

Teachers with strong classroom management often nip poor behaviour in the bud well before it has had a chance to escalate and reach the stage where a sanction becomes necessary. There are a number of things that you can try.

Have a quick word

Let's say that you have a chatty pupil who isn't belligerent but keeps talking after several warnings. Instead of doing the usual (three warnings followed by a sanction), after a couple of warnings, say, 'Can you wait outside? I'd like to have a quick word.' Leave them outside for a minute or two, and then attend to them and say, 'What do you think I want to speak to you about?' Most pupils will acknowledge their misbehaviour, at which point say something to the effect of, 'I know you can be good when you want to be. But at the moment, you're giving me no other choice but to set you a detention.' Having a word with them outside removes the audience – which some kids love – and the perceived reluctance to set a detention tells the child that you're a perfectly reasonable person who is not out for blood; rather, consequences are dictated by actions.

Phone home

Normally, phoning home is done as a sanction in its own right. There is no reason why, however, you can't make a *warning* phone call home before a sanction even becomes necessary. For example, let's say that you have a child who stops misbehaving after you've given them two warnings, but in doing so still causes significant disruption. Instead of setting a detention, phone home and tell the parent/guardian, 'He's a good lad, but he just talks too much and it's making the learning difficult for the rest of the class. If it continues, I'm sure you understand that I'll have to do something about it.' Once you've spoken to the parent, speak to the child and reiterate the same message. In most cases, even the most disruptive child is humbled – let alone embarrassed – when on the phone to a teacher with their parents/guardians watching. If nothing else, they'll behave to avoid you ringing them again!

Have a meeting

This is usually effective with a child who – for whatever reason – has decided that they hate your guts and is outright hostile. You will likely have sanctioned them a few times before, so the aim of the meeting is to avoid *further* sanctions. All you have to do is request a meeting with the child and a pastoral lead, stating that you feel there has been a breakdown in communication between you and the child. In the meeting itself, do not ask the child a series of inane questions – 'What were you thinking when you did XYZ? What have you thought about since? How did it make you feel?' – as this is not a restorative conversation. Don't demand an apology either and for heaven's sake don't go apologising to the child if they start blaming you for something. Instead, redirect the conversation and make it clear to the child that you don't dislike them by pointing out some good trait in their personality: 'You could be a good leader if you wanted to be' or 'I can see that you're a very good friend to many of the kids in the class'. Poorly behaved pupils often have good personality traits (sense of humour, loyalty, directness, confidence, etc.) but they just use them in the wrong way. Make sure that you separate the two and tell them how brilliant they could be if they used their skills appropriately. Finish by making your expectations clear in the same way as before: 'If your behaviour doesn't improve, you leave me with no choice but to keep sending you out. It would be such a shame. I don't want that. Neither do you. Be the person we all know you can be.' The pastoral lead will mostly remain quiet or chip in to support you where appropriate, but it is worth emailing them beforehand outlining the direction in which you'd like the meeting to go.

The pace of your lesson

One of the main areas that new teachers struggle with in their teaching is lesson pace. While interpretations vary in specifics, a good pace essentially involves maximising learning time, and one of the biggest killers of pace is low-level disruption. When planning your lesson, however, if you think about its technicalities as well as how you're going to use your resources, much of this can be eliminated. What kids will take full advantage of – and therefore what you need to avoid – is often referred to as 'dead time', i.e. times in the lesson when nothing is happening. For example, let's say that you're getting the kids to watch a video, after which you will hand out some questions. Commonly what will happen is that the kids will watch the video and then the video will finish, at which point you will start handing out your sheets. It is during this time – dead time – that the kids will start talking and you will have to waste time getting them quiet again. Instead, then, hand all your sheets out at the start (before the kids even get there if possible) face down. When the video finishes, say, 'Right. Can you turn over the sheet in front of you? You've got six minutes to answer the questions. In silence please. Go!' Apply the same logic when handing out glue sticks (if you're lucky enough to have some), changing slideshows or anything else that would interrupt the flow of your lesson.

When meeting a class for the first time

The phrase 'don't smile until Christmas' is perhaps the most debated idea within behaviour management. Like many old wives' tales, it may not be 100 per cent true, but there is definitely some truth in it. To maintain order in your classroom, you don't have to forfeit all human emotion until Christmas, but being 'stricter' at the start of the year pays no end of dividends for the rest thereof. I have spoken to hundreds of NQTs who regret being relaxed early on, but never – literally never – have I encountered an NQT who felt the opposite. When meeting your class for the first time, consider doing some of what follows – again, only if it resonates.

The seating plan

Your school will most probably insist that you have one and will likely give you some guidance with which to appoint particular seats to particular pupils. In any case, a seating plan is highly recommended and what is just as important is *how* you go about putting your pupils in the seating plan. When they enter your classroom, ask them to line up along the back and stand in silence with their jackets off, etc. Neither smile nor frown; remain expressionless. Call your kids one by one and direct them to their appointed seat, at which there should be some simple task ready for them to do, e.g. writing their name or class, on the cover of their new books. Don't call out the next pupil until the current pupil has sat down, and insist on silence throughout. Don't project the seating plan on the screen and say, 'Right. Can we all find our places and sit down?' They may well comply and it's by no means bad practice, but it is important that you establish yourself in the first meeting, and one of the most effective ways of doing this – as harsh as it may sound – is by exercising as much control over the situation as possible. In addition, this method will help you to identify potentially disruptive pupils, as very few will challenge a teacher in the first lesson. If you do get any who refuse to sit in the seating plan, maintain an expressionless face and politely but assertively say, 'You will need to sit here for now.' (Of course, the 'for now' is a lie, deliberately told so that the kids will know you have a 'good' side. Remember when Mary Poppins said that 'a spoonful of sugar helps the medicine go down'? As she too was dealing with kids, what she should have said was, 'A little bit of bullshit helps the truth go down.' Once you've established good behaviour, never, ever change the seating plan to allow kids to sit next to their friends of choice.)

The rules

Once the kids are sat down in their new seats, project your rules on the screen and ask pupils to copy them – again, in silence. Keep them brief – no more than six – and focus on behaviours that would adversely affect learning, i.e. prioritise rules like 'I will not talk when Miss Smith is talking' or 'I will complete all classwork to the best of my ability' over 'I will not chew gum in class'. While pupils are copying, explain that the rules are there for their benefit, and without them learning cannot take place. Tell them that now you've discussed the rules and they're written in their books, you would like never to have to refer to them again. Nine times out of ten, your class will comply with this ritual but it is important at this stage that you *not* give them any praise, as doing so would suggest that you're somewhat surprised. Rather, act like it's perfectly normal for your expectations to be followed and nothing for you or them to be excited about (see Chapter 9).

Maintain an imbalance

Yes, you read that correctly. For the first three weeks (or longer if your gut tells you) remain as robotic and emotionless as you were in the first lesson. If kids see too much of your human side too soon, they will very likely begin to push boundaries: 'Sir's safe!' they'll tell each other. In any case, the consequences of relaxing too soon are far greater than those of being too 'strict' for too long, so the latter makes far more sense. As 'don't smile until Christmas' is often wrongly interpreted as 'be as shouty and as unapproachable as you can until Christmas', it is worth noting here that the latter is not at all being suggested. Being confrontational is counterproductive (let alone unprofessional), and unapproachability will hinder pupil progress and will ultimately make the kids hate you. The reason for being tactically and temporarily emotionless is that, in doing so, your rules are doubly emphasised because your demeanour is a constant reflection of them. There is a reason why the police don't stand around giggling, etc. and always keep their composure when on duty.

Would you feel safe if they didn't? So just wait a bit before you show off your dazzling personality.

As well as being emotionally reserved to begin with, the other imbalance that you should maintain concerns the types of activities that you build into your lessons. During the same initial time period and for the exact same reasons, you want to aim for pin-drop silence for the bulk of every lesson. Keep the group work, discussions, etc. significantly lower than you would probably like to, and if the work does involve talking, keep it short and snappy, i.e. 'Discuss XYZ for one minute. Go!' As every teacher's biggest behaviour issue is low-level disruption, training your kids to be silent when asked will prevent future group work or other discussion activities descending into chaos. (NB: it is fully appreciated that this might not be possible for your specific subject, in which case the key message in the first few weeks is to not let kids talk unless the work necessitates it. After that, you'll be better able to allow the kids to have a quiet chat now and again while working.)

A warning on behaviour

Another problem with the education system – and consequently schools – is that all too often, either because they're unaware, they're too busy or they don't care enough, school leaders wait until absolute breaking point before they intervene.

Let's say that you've got a class that has six or seven 'key players' who are hell-bent on ruining your lesson by being extremely disruptive themselves or by 'egging on' otherwise well-behaved pupils. Whatever you try just does not seem to work and every lesson is the same: the moment that you start speaking, you are interrupted several times and learning doesn't start for at least 15 minutes into the lesson, the remainder of which you spend putting what seems like thousands of warnings on the board. Nothing works. You dread teaching the class and you can feel them getting to you on an emotional level. One Friday afternoon you reach breaking point and burst into tears in the middle of your lesson – right in front of the kids.

Firstly, have no doubt in your mind about how common the above situation is. The only thing that you can do from your side to try to avoid it is spotting it – and therefore reporting it – early. Unfortunately, what often happens is that the teacher is either in denial about how much a 'bad' class has affected them so they just stay quiet or they are too embarrassed to ask for help because they work with too many arseholes who smugly say stuff like, 'Well, they behave in my lesson.'

Dear teachers, if you ever feel that a class has got to you emotionally, don't let it chip away at you for weeks before you tell someone. As well as the adverse effects that doing so could have on your wellbeing, emotional reactions can be detrimental to your career. To some kids, making a teacher cry is a badge of honour. So if senior leaders don't take immediate measures, the behaviour of said class may worsen and so might the behaviour of other classes that you teach (if you're secondary). As well as this – and particularly if it happens more than once – you might find yourself feeling like you're being told off for crying. Rightly or wrongly, in the eyes of school leaders, a teacher crying in the presence of pupils is bad for *the pupils'* emotional health and wellbeing, so school leaders may well address it in a way that makes it entirely your problem.

Emotional reactions, by the way, are by no means limited to crying. We all know that while one person may cry, another person in the exact same situation may scream, punch a wall or just sit and stare into space. A teacher once had a class similar to the one described above. After constantly being interrupted for 30 minutes straight, he slammed his hand on the desk and screamed, 'DO YOU WANT TO FUCKING PASS OR NOT?!!' Luckily for him there was no complaint from the kids but, just in case, he went to the head of his own accord and confessed. The head did the right thing and checked up on his wellbeing, asked him whether he needed time off, etc., as well as giving him a (hard) slap on the wrist. He was very lucky: had the kids complained to their parents and the parents complained to the school, it could have gone down very differently.

On a side note, while it is not being suggested that swearing in front of your class is a trivial matter, it is worth noting that, more often than not, kids are actually very forgiving of momentary errors in judgement that don't adversely affect them directly – even more so when they have a good relationship with the teacher. Teaching, however, has more than its fair share of busybodies: the annoying, know-it-all, self-righteous teacher in the room next door is way more likely to report you for missing a marking episode than a kid is for you accidentally playing a song with inappropriate lyrics. Seriously, how hard is it to mind your own business?

Summary

- For all practical purposes, there are three types of behaviour policy: the consequence system, restorative practice and zero tolerance. Different versions of the consequence system are the most common. Zero tolerance is rare and restorative practice (without sanctions) is ineffective.
- The common problem is that pupil behaviour is considered to be the teacher's responsibility, but if you are overly reliant on a behaviour management system, you will be seen as a weak teacher.
- In order to avoid using the behaviour system, work on three things: your teacher voice, by developing a variety of distinctly different tones; your body language, by adopting good posture and always appearing calm; and your teacher space, by occupying different parts of your classroom while teaching.
- Prioritise dealing with misbehaviours that adversely affect learning – this will most probably be low-level disruption. Don't make a big deal out of misbehaviours for the sake of it or out of principle. Be pragmatic.
- Stop poor behaviour getting to the point where you need to issue a sanction by having a 'quick word' with the child outside the room, phoning home or having a mediated meeting with the child. Maintain a well-paced lesson with little or no 'dead time' to minimise low-level disruption.
- When meeting a class for the first time, it is important that you exercise as much control as possible. Have a seating plan and direct pupils to their seats one by one. Get them to copy your rules in silence immediately afterwards. To maintain a silent classroom, for the first few weeks avoid tasks that involve prolonged discussions.
- Emotional outbursts over misbehaviour are usually the product of repeated gross misbehaviour over long periods of time. If you ever feel that a class has got to you on an emotional level, it is important that you identify it early and get the support that you need, lest you end up doing something that you will later regret.

Chapter 9
How to use rewards effectively

As well as using sanctions to discourage poor behaviour/achievement, schools use rewards and encourage teachers to praise their pupils in order to recognise their achievements and keep them motivated. For the most part, the education system has got it right: in the crude sense, most humans will go the extra mile to gain pleasure or avoid pain. Kids are no different. It makes perfect sense for the education system to respond to the human mindset.

The problems, however, relate to the way in which the system – and consequently schools – uses rewards/praise. Over-rewarding, under-rewarding, rewarding the 'wrong' pupils and ignoring the 'right' pupils seem to be themes across schools. If you ever get a chance to conduct some pupil voice surveys, pick some of your consistently well-behaved, high-effort-making pupils and ask them whether they agree with the last sentence.

The problem with rewards

Rewarding the basics

For reasons beyond the scope of this chapter – and indeed even this book – the education system is disproportionately focused on narrowing 'gaps'. In other words, whatever the area – behaviour, attendance or achievement – the system seeks to get pupils who aren't meeting a particular (arbitrary) standard to meet said standard. The by-product of this is that pupils who are not doing what can be described as 'the basics' become the focal point of a school's efforts.

If you have a poorly behaved class, no doubt one of the first things that school leaders will tell you to do is be positive, praise them at every opportunity and/or be generous with rewards. In a bid to get your class where you want them, you'll follow this advice and find that any success you have with them is temporary, i.e. after you reward them for one or two lessons of peace, you'll find that they go back to normal. Kids, like adults, are often extrinsically motivated, so by rewarding them too soon or for something not particularly significant, they infer that they've achieved whatever is necessary and so cease to make an effort, essentially putting the teacher in a situation where it's 'reward us or else'.

The system encourages teachers to reward pupils for meeting basic standards. Not only is it ineffective but it is also counterproductive: when well-behaved pupils see that all you have to do is sit in a chair to get a merit point, you'll soon find them out of their seat more often. In addition to this, pupils who pretty much always meet basic standards are often ignored and have a legitimate gripe with the system for this. If you'd never been sent out of the room as a pupil but a pupil who got sent out every few lessons got to go on a trip (that you didn't) when they stopped getting sent out, you'd be a bit pissed off too, surely?

The same is true for attendance. A kid who hasn't had a day off all term will be ignored completely at worst and at best will be given nowhere near the same level of praise/reward as a child who went from 60 per cent to 85 per cent attendance in a half-term. Same with achievement: a kid who does very little in class for weeks on end and suddenly improves is given far more praise than a child who always tries their best.

Forced rewards

Another problem is the lack of teacher ownership over rewards. As well as being encouraged or outright told what to reward, often there is a reward quota that has to be met by a certain time period. Your school may, for example, give teachers a fixed number of tokens that they *have* to distribute in a given half-term to pupils who will later exchange them for cash/prizes. In some schools you may be told to issue three merit points per lesson, and at others you may *have* to give an 'effort award' to one pupil every half-term and won't be allowed to use the same pupil twice. The same concept is applied to marking policies, many of which require teachers to state at least one positive aspect by describing 'what went well' or 'two stars' before they suggest areas for improvement – 'even better if' or 'a wish'. It's a nice idea, but if a kid blatantly made no effort and got 4/30 in a test, surely the four marks that they did get could probably be better described as a product of luck rather than 'what went well'? Is it absolutely necessary to desperately clutch to and praise the one thing that you wouldn't have even noticed if the marking policy didn't tell you to? Surely if it went *that* well you wouldn't have to look for it?

All of this is probably well meant, but there are three negative consequences of such a 'box-ticking' type of system. Firstly, you inevitably end up rewarding/praising undeserving pupils, which is morally wrong. Secondly, off the back of that, you risk enabling a child's contentment with lower standards (4/30 is unacceptable – yet you're giving them 'two stars' before the 'wish'?). And thirdly, when quotas or robust policies are involved, rewards are more likely to be issued in a robotic, disingenuous way, risking the diminishment of their effect.

In essence, the education system's concept of rewards bears little resemblance to reality: nowhere else is one rewarded for meeting basic standards. Nowhere else do people go to great lengths to find someone to reward. Nowhere else does one receive a reward because the giver was told to choose someone. In most real-world scenarios, rewards require sustained effort and outstanding achievement. Of course, we are dealing with kids, so their reality cannot and should not reflect ours entirely (we'd have to make them contribute to rent or mortgage payments too if that was the case), but if the aim of school is to prepare kids for the 'real world', what goes on at school needs to resemble it at least a tad more than it currently does.

You, as the teacher, can do a lot to improve this part of the system.

Who, what and how to reward

Don't reward the basics

It goes without saying that you have to follow your school's rewards policy. Whatever it may be, you will still have a significant amount of leeway when it comes to deciding who to – and who not to – reward.

There are some pupils for whom the basics are a genuine struggle. For reasons beyond the scope of this book, some pupils simply do not have good attendance, struggle to behave and cannot see the value of education. If you're experienced, your professional judgement will tell you exactly who these pupils are, but in any case, school pastoral leads regularly share information with teachers, and obviously teachers are well aware of pupils' individual learning needs. For such pupils, the rewarding of basics is not only recommended but necessary. Schools have a duty to nurture as well as prepare kids for the 'real world'.

It is not the case, however, that every child who doesn't get it right is not doing so due to some significantly adverse external factor(s): many kids are disengaged, misbehave or miss school for no reason that would reduce you to tears. For these pupils, be very frugal if/when rewarding the basics. Generally speaking, either don't reward them at all or only reward when the said standard has been met consistently over a long period of time. After two good lessons with a poorly behaved class, don't fall for the trap of saying yes when a kid puts their hand up and says, 'Miss, we've behaved really well today. Can we have five minutes' free time in the lesson?' If you say yes, you can guarantee that their behaviour either won't be as good next lesson or will require the same or greater reward to make it so.

The same applies for basic standards in attendance and achievement. For both your sake and the kids', act neither happy nor unhappy when basic standards are met in the short term. You have to give kids the impression that you are *used* to your expectations being met and, for this reason, it is nothing for you to be excited about as it's nothing out of the ordinary for a dedicated teacher like you.

Reward the kids who always get it right

As the culture of the education system dictates that we reward improvements in standards more than we reward consistently high standards, pupils of the latter description are often under-praised or outright ignored. For the classroom teacher, as such pupils are usually quiet, well-behaved and not overly demanding of your attention, it can be easy to take them for granted and inadvertently treat them unfairly by not giving them credit where credit is due. There is no need to state the obvious by telling you what to do to overcome this, but just try to remember that high standards – even if they seemingly come more naturally to some pupils – still require effort, and we are doing a disservice to our pupils if we don't reward them. It's just about being aware and avoiding being so caught up with the demands of the system that you lose sight of your greater purpose as a teacher.

How to praise/reward

As stated earlier, the desired effect of rewards (which are ultimately motivation and recognition) can be diminished when they are issued in a robotic, disingenuous way: 'Well done. Here's the house point I have to give you.' For many pupils, a lack of recognition is more bothersome than a lack of a tangible reward. That being the case, in addition to giving rewards, give pupils credit by being very particular in how you give them verbal praise. After consistently high achievement in a particular subject, for example, you could keep them behind at the end of the lesson and not only tell them how impressed you are, but also say something to the effect of 'This is the kind of work that's going to get you very far in life.' Say it with a warm tone and watch their reaction. Rewards serve their purpose far better when they are accompanied by the sincerity of warm praise. To give a child the recognition that they deserve, phone home and tell the parent/guardian the same thing you told the pupil. (Phoning home is perhaps the most effective but underused way of giving a child recognition. If ever there was a time to get over your fear of talking on the phone, this is it!) In essence, for the betterment of your pupils, make a conscious effort not to let the demands of the system make you robotic. The words of a good teacher are far more impactful than some stupid sticker.

Summary

- Schools use sanctions and rewards to manage behaviour and achievement.
- As schools seek to reward improvement, basics (attendance, complying with simple instructions, etc.) are often rewarded. This is either ineffective or counterproductive. It also demoralises pupils who are consistently good in these areas.
- Rewards are often issued in a forced way. For example, there may be reward quotas or compulsory issuing of rewards in a given half-term. When issued in such a way, the wrong pupil ends up being rewarded and pupils may end up feeling content with lower standards.
- Don't reward the basics unless absolutely necessary. Some pupils fail to meet basic standards due to external – sometimes upsetting – circumstances. For these pupils, it is necessary to reward the basics.
- Recognise and reward pupils who always get it right. Not doing so is an injustice.
- Verbal praise can be far more effective than a stamp, sticker, etc. as long as it is given in the correct way. Display your sincerity by adopting a warm tone and be very specific in what you say.

Chapter 10

How to build positive relationships with your pupils

Whether it's behaviour management or otherwise getting the best out of your pupils, all aspects of your teaching will be significantly better if the relationship you have with your kids is a positive one. Even I – as someone who naturally engaged with academia and mostly avoided trouble – can think of teachers for whom I behaved better or worse when I was a pupil based on all sorts of reasons, which I then couldn't pinpoint. So, what was it about those particular teachers that meant that their pupils looked forward to their lessons and were almost always on board? And, more importantly, why is it essential that you know and adapt these characteristics?

The problems with relationships

The education system – and consequently schools – is correct in encouraging teachers to build relationships with their pupils. In itself, this is a positive. The problem, however, is that more often than not, they tell teachers to do so, fail to teach them how and then blame them when they don't. When a teacher is struggling with an 'underachieving' or misbehaving pupil, for example, it is not uncommon for their concerns to be dismissed with 'Well, it's down to you to build a relationship with them.' With little or no further guidance, the teacher ends up feeling demoralised and confused.

To be fair to school leaders, teachers are rightly encouraged to show compassion, empathy, humour, etc., but rarely is any specific guidance on what to *say* and *do* when in the classroom to best enable positive relationships given. As a result, some new teachers end up being too pally with the kids while others become excessively authoritarian – both of which are detrimental to good practice. Unfortunately for some, the consequent feeling of blame leads to an unbearable sense of disillusionment.

In any case, having a good relationship with your pupils will not only soften the blows from some parts of the education system, but it will also lead to greater job satisfaction. Surely you want your kids to smile when they think of you in 20 years' time?

How to build positive relationships with your pupils

Irrelevant chat

Once your behaviour expectations have been established, talk to your kids. Obviously, you're hardly going to have been silent before that time but this is referring to talking that is neither about the work nor otherwise instructional. Let's say, for example, that you're four weeks into term with your new class and you've got them where you want them in terms of your expectations. Now is a good time for you to show some of your human side. Every so often, make a point of going around your class and talking to pupils individually about something entirely unrelated to your lesson. It could be about football, music, TV shows, etc. The topic is actually not that important and by no means do you have to be 'down with the kids' for this to be effective. What is important, however, is *how* you talk. To allow your genuineness to radiate, lose your teacher voice altogether and speak to your kids the way in which you would speak to your colleagues in the staffroom if the headteacher was present. In other words, if your tone was an item of clothing, it should be considered 'smart-casual'. Be friendly, but don't try to be friends. If topics for conversation don't come naturally to you, just listen to the pupils' chatter and chip in with your two pence. Soon enough they'll start asking you questions either way. Some of the bigger personalities in the class may even instigate a friendly debate over something, in which case by all means argue against them with the whole class watching!

As well as building a good relationship with your kids generally, this is also a good time to build a relationship with 'naughty' pupils specifically. Let's say, for example, that you had to remove the same pupil three times for constant disruption. Now is the perfect opportunity for you to build that relationship with them, consequently getting them to do their best in all aspects of your lessons. Generally speaking, sharing common interests works particularly well with such pupils, so if you support the same football team, now is a good time to talk about it.

When engaging in irrelevant chat, you have to be very controlled. Again, make sure that your classroom management is solid first. In any case, if you spend too much time talking about who should have been picked by whom on some reality TV show, kids will see you as more of a mate (mates are not an authority over mates) and the standards in your classroom will dip. Don't let it go on for longer than a few minutes and if ever the kids are getting too loud, suddenly clap your hands and shout, 'Right! Let's get this done. Five minutes please. NO talking.' Also, be careful of pupils who will try to lure you into an irrelevant discussion in order to avoid work. For example, if pupils know that you're an Aston Villa fan, some might interrupt you while you're teaching photosynthesis: 'Miss, did you see Villa on Saturday?' This can be difficult as you don't want to be rude, so just say something to the effect of, 'I did. But we can talk about it later. A plant needs carbon dioxide, water...' If the standards (behaviour or otherwise) in your class dip, then, after giving your class the 'I'm so disappointed' speech, suspend all irrelevant chat until they're back where you want them.

Break and lunchtime duty are also a good – if not better – time for irrelevant chats as there are fewer time constraints. When you're on duty, as a minimum, greet the pupils if you bump into them and if *they* initiate conversation, do as above. If you decide to initiate, keep it brief: while kids will appreciate you talking to them, they won't want to waste their entire breaktime talking to a teacher. On a side note, if you are new to a school, the greater the number of kids that know your face, the easier it will be to establish yourself. Don't petition for me to be kicked out of the union for suggesting this, but consider doing an extra break/lunch duty so that you can walk around raising your profile. (For the love of God, don't tell SLT that you're doing more duties than you should be! You don't want them forcing you to do more next year.)

Humour

Being funny and having a good sense of humour will not only enable better relationships with pupils but possessing these traits will also make your career much more enjoyable overall. The only problem (if you consider it a problem) is that neither of the aforementioned can be taught. Some people are funny by nature and others are less so. Just like any other trait advantageous to teaching that you may possess (like being upbeat or confident in social situations, for example), use whatever humour you have to your advantage. Be it corny, immature or dry, throwing it into your lessons at the appropriate times will pay you no end of dividends.

Just like the irrelevant chats, humour should be used in a controlled way and it is probably best to avoid it at the start of a lesson, particularly with a challenging group, as the last thing that you want to do is set them off before they even start. Again, only do it once your classroom management is solid and rein it in if the standards slip.

Along with unfairness, one of the most disliked traits by pupils in a teacher is that of arrogance or self-importance. Yes, every red-blooded teacher loves the sound of their own voice and we all probably have an imposing personality to some degree, but if kids get the impression that you think you are better than them, be assured that they will hate you. One obvious way around this is by... wait for it... not being arrogant. Don't get me wrong – you're most probably not, but often kids get the wrong impression of someone in authority. To avoid this, the best type of humour to inject in your lessons is self-deprecating humour, as people who laugh at themselves rarely consider themselves above others.

In any case, such teachers are much more likely to be 'forgiven' by pupils when they inevitably do something to piss them off (not letting them go to the toilet, sanctioning them for not doing homework or keeping the whole class in at break when only seven kids were talking, to name but a few examples). So make a point of laughing at yourself every now and then. Not too long ago, a girl in my class said that she 'needed' a new book, despite her book still having a good handful of pages left. She kept insisting, 'Sir, I NEED a new book.' I eventually got fed up of saying no and told her, 'I NEED a full head of hair, but you don't get everything you want in life, do you?!' I'm convinced that it's because of little things like this that I had such a good relationship with the class. (When used cleverly with the right pupil, humour can also be used to diffuse a potential altercation.)

As fun and as helpful as self-deprecating humour can be, do be careful: if you overuse it, kids will see you as someone to be laughed at and may end up making fun of you in the wrong way and at the wrong times. They may even tell their friends how 'safe' you are, and even kids that you don't teach might try it. In that event, switch back to the tone you used in your first lesson and keep the culprits behind to have a quick word.

Empathy, compassion, etc.

Earlier we mentioned that pupils respond better to teachers who show traits such as empathy, compassion, impartiality, etc. While this is all well and good, by their very nature you don't get to show that you have these traits on a daily basis – at least not directly. When is the last time you showed a kid that you're non-judgemental and empathic? If you had to think about it, it clearly isn't that often – through no fault of your own, of course. Kids, like adults, make inferences: when you meet and greet them at the door, when you have an irrelevant chat, when you remember that your football team beat theirs on the weekend and when you make fun of yourself, you give off the vibes of an emotionally intelligent person who has a genuine interest in them as people. Nothing enables relationship-building better than that.

To be or not to be liked

If someone asked you what you think of your five closest friends, no doubt you would be able to sing their praises to anyone and everyone and probably couldn't imagine how your life would be without them. You would be lying to yourself, however, if you said that there wasn't a single 'negative' trait about them that does your head in from time to time. Most of us have a need to be liked (this is nothing to be ashamed of and is perhaps essential to our survival) but it is important that we maintain perspective. If the majority of people had to describe their friends, family or colleagues, they'd say something to the effect of, 'I love so and so to bits. But they can be a bit [insert annoying trait].' When behaving authentically, rarely is anyone entirely liked.

I always find it fascinating how much children know what's good for them. One would assume that kids would like a relaxed or 'safe' teacher who allows them to talk all lesson with their headphones in, has low academic expectations and never sets detentions. While such teachers are obviously rare, the novelty of even a less 'safe' teacher wears off very quickly. If you don't believe me, take two weeks off and see how annoyed your class gets in the second week with a supply teacher who happens to be 'safe'. Be assured that while the kids may *want* to just have fun, they *need* structure and discipline. And they know that they do. (NB: It is not being suggested here that all – or even a significant minority of – supply teachers are 'safe'. Rather, the example shows that, sometimes, the true value of a good teacher is only really known in their absence.)

If you're a new teacher, you're probably balancing your desire to be liked by your pupils with the need to be respected by them. What the previous scenario indicates is that the two are intertwined: in the end, they will not like you if your standards are low. With this in mind, aim to be neither entirely liked nor entirely disliked. In other words, be the teacher version of all of your closest friends. Behind your back, you want your kids to say stuff like 'Sir's a sick teacher but he can be a right bastard sometimes' or 'I'm serious. Miss fully does my head in. Legit, though – she cares about us.' In this sense, our job allows us to be authentic: embrace your authenticity by not compromising your high standards for fear of being disliked. It won't work anyway!

Being liked by the pupils is not essential (by and large, disliked teachers still get the job done) but – and this is a big 'but' – your life and the kids' lives will be a whole lot easier if they do like you in the way described above. Invest time building relationships, use the strength of your personality and where you fear that you may be 'lacking' in a particular trait, e.g. bubbliness or humour, show the important traits that you do possess, e.g. empathy and compassion, at every opportunity.

Summary

- Whether it's behaviour management or otherwise getting the best out of your pupils, all aspects of your teaching will be significantly better if the relationship that you have with your kids is a positive one.
- The education system acknowledges the importance of these relationships; however, schools do not effectively teach staff how to build them. Because of the lack of guidance, many teachers end up becoming excessively authoritarian or excessively pally with their pupils – both of which are detrimental to a teacher's practice.
- You can build positive relationships with your pupils by chatting (on occasion) about matters unrelated to the lesson during the lesson itself. You must do this in a very controlled way, as kids will take advantage. Humour – particularly self-deprecating humour – also helps to build relationships. It is during these interactions that your empathy and compassion are inferred by your pupils.
- Seek to be neither liked nor disliked by your pupils. Unconsciously, kids can distinguish between what they like and what is good for them, so they don't respect teachers who lower their standards for the sake of being liked. They know that maintaining order requires you to annoy them on occasion, so it is inevitable that they will dislike you from time to time. They know this. You know this. It's all good.

Chapter 11

How to get the support you need

The supply–demand mismatch

One of the biggest complaints from new teachers is the lack of support available in their early years of teaching. The education system, it seems, is responsible for two errors: firstly, an error in perception – new teachers are seemingly unaware of the level and type of support available to them – and secondly, not as much time is invested in new teachers as perhaps it should be. Naturally, the consequent feeling of disheartenment leads to a sense of disillusion. It is therefore important for new teachers to a) have a balanced view of the support available to them and b) more importantly, know how to get the support that they desire.

What support is and what it isn't

There is a fine line between asking for support and asking someone to do something for you. If I ask you to mark my tests, this is not asking for support as it's entirely you doing the work and not me. But if I ask you for strategies to get through my pile quicker and you tell me to mark them one question at a time, then you should receive no end of thanks for your support. If I lose my shit and send a kid to your room within five minutes of the start of my lesson, all I've done is transfer my problem to you, so it's not really support that you've provided me with. If, however, you advise me on how best to deal with a kid who arrives to the lesson late with an attitude problem, then… I'm sure you get the idea.

Now we've cleared that up, allow me just to clarify. There are times when you may need higher levels of support, e.g. a pupil removing immediately or your workload reduced, but this type of support is usually only given as a last resort. Irrespective of how much a school may tell you how supportive it is, only expect them to outright do something major for you as a final option.

How to get the support you need

Of course, there are those who fully understand the nature of support, but they too often complain about a lack thereof. The simple fact is that, as mentioned earlier, the system does not invest as much time in new teachers as it perhaps should. In other words, the reason why we often don't get the support we need is because the person who is meant to be supporting us does not have the time to do so. They will most likely want to give you lots of support and will feel guilty about not providing it, but for them too, there are only 24 hours in a day and, like you, they are very probably teaching a full timetable.

Nonetheless, it is perfectly normal to need support in the early stages of your career and, at any school worth working at, there is no stigma attached. When you apply the strategies that follow, do so with the knowledge that the best way to get what you want in an educational setting is through enthusiasm and proactivity. Grumpy demands are rarely met and, even if they are, they will at best portray you in a negative light, and at worst place a target on your head. It is worth noting that, due to the high level of emotional labour involved in the job, it is very easy for a teacher to fall into negativity (or at least what can be perceived as negativity). A teacher who doesn't have a game plan and/or struggles with emotional self-control can easily morph from Miss Honey to Arthur Shelby in one half-term. (NB: If *lots* of teachers become angry and annoyed in a particular school, then it's SLT that needs support, not them.)

As well as helping you to get the support that you need, applying the following strategies will do wonders for your professional reputation.

Support is a bit like sympathy – it runs out

You know that one friend who's always got some big drama and seems to constantly be getting screwed over? You may well have known them since sixth-form but as nice, warm and caring as you are, they will eventually do your head in. You'll wonder why the hell they can't deal with anything themselves and will either tell them to put a sock in it or just start ignoring their texts. Like sympathy, support requires time and energy – both of which are limited, no matter how much we may wish otherwise. Constantly needing support will also make you appear less competent in the eyes of school leaders. There is one golden rule: if you can do it yourself and/or it is not *serious*, don't ask for support. So, if you've forgotten how to enter your reports, don't go sending pesky emails to your head of department in the middle of the night. Rather, find out when a fellow teacher is doing theirs, then sit with them and do yours. If the last person who taught in your room changed the layout without changing it back, speak to them directly before you go snitching. In essence, don't bother those 'above' you with triviality. Save the support for when you need it.

Control the meeting

If you're an NQT, you will have weekly meetings scheduled. If that is the case, while it is important to let off steam and have a general chat with your mentor, do use the time effectively to get the support that you need: 'This week I've tried the following activities. I think I need to do more… What do you think would work with this group?' is how your conversations should go. If you don't have a meeting scheduled – in any case, not everything can be delayed until the meeting – try to avoid just turning up at someone's door and listing everything that's giving you palpitations. Don't get me wrong, they'll probably still provide you with *some* support in this scenario, but they too will most probably be busy! If you want the maximum level of support, say, 'When is/Is now a good time to talk about XYZ?' By going about it this way, not only are you showing that you're respectful of the time of others, but whoever is supporting you will also be able to offer you more time. It is better to speak to people in person wherever possible but there is no harm in putting the above in an email.

First support yourself

Let's say that you've got a class that is highly compliant with behaviour rules but doesn't seem to engage much with the learning. No matter what you do they just seem to stare into space, never raise their hands, work at a slow pace – you get the picture. When you're finally fed up, instead of asking your mentor, 'How the hell am I meant to get them to make progress?', say (and make sure that you've actually done) something to the effect of, 'I've tried using rewards. I even promised to ring home for the kid that finished first. They just don't seem interested.' – to which a good mentor will reply with something like, 'Have you tried using songs? How about videos?' By stating what you have already tried, not only are you portraying yourself as an independent, competent professional, but your enthusiasm will also radiate and those above you will be more willing to prioritise your professional development.

Be careful with readily available support

Your school will have some sort of shared area (which will no doubt be a chaotic mess) from which you can use existing lesson plans and resources and upload the same. Your school may also have a behaviour policy that is easily applicable and doesn't involve much work from the teacher. It goes without saying that both of these are good things in and of themselves, but you should not become reliant on them. Obviously, there is no harm in using the resources from the shared area – the entire purpose of a shared area is to reduce teacher workload – but if you're simply lifting lessons/resources without tweaking them to suit your learners' needs, well then, you're doing it wrong. Teachers who arrive at school at 8.37 am and manically start clicking through slideshows that they've never seen before usually don't do so well. The same goes for the teachers who are constantly setting detentions or kicking kids out of the lesson. By its very definition, support – even readily available support – serves primarily as a backup.

Chain of command

Like any organisation, a school has a hierarchy of power. The headteacher doesn't mop the corridors and teachers don't do bulk photocopying... Oh wait. Jokes aside, be aware that the hierarchy of power is also a hierarchy of support: just because someone is above you in the hierarchy, it doesn't mean that it's *their* support you're entitled to. If you're an NQT, for example, don't go straight to the deputy head for support with a difficult class and don't ask your middle leader to explain the marking policy, as both of these are primarily the job of your mentor. (Make sure that you know who's responsible for what, as it does vary from school to school.) By making sure that you ask the right person the right things, you will avoid being fobbed off and, more importantly, you will get the maximum level of support available.

A note on CPD

Due to either a lack of money or a lack of time, it is common for teachers to complain of not getting the CPD they desire. Again, in this respect, the system does not seem to invest as much time in new teachers as it should. To be fair to schools, many *do* develop their staff effectively despite external factors, but nonetheless, the aforementioned feeling is all too common. Luckily, the barrier of time and money can be worked around – at least to some extent.

In my experience, the best possible professional development that a teacher can get is not from attending a workshop or listening to a speaker (although I'm not knocking these), nor is it from reading books on pedagogy (I'm not knocking these either). Rather, the best CPD can be acquired from simply talking to other teachers. You will be surprised how many strategies, activities, etc. you can pick up just from asking colleagues about how they would teach a given topic. Savvier schools have caught on, but most schools don't give teachers the time – or at least sufficient time – to exchange ideas.

The advice here is simple: speak to your colleagues. Observing them can be helpful, but simply asking them *what they do* in any area in which you feel you need support will do wonders for your CPD. The good thing about teachers is that we are inherently supportive people and I'd be lying if I said that we don't love the sound of our own voices. So ask away! Remember at the same time, however, that many of us are, perhaps paradoxically, inclined to stubbornness (many of us believe that our way is the only correct way) and fear of judgement. So always begin your sentence with, 'Here's what *I* do…' when someone asks, and if someone relates a strategy that you think is absolutely ludicrous, keep your mouth shut and remember that what works for one teacher may not work for another.

So, if this is so easy, why aren't people already doing it? Well, they are in pockets, but what normally happens is that because schools are so fast paced, the immediate becomes priority. Out of necessity, teachers mostly talk about what's about to happen (upcoming assessments, reports, meetings, behaviour, etc.) or use what little free time we have to engage in light-hearted banter, which is also essential. Nonetheless, I am convinced that if we all dedicated just a few minutes every couple of days, we could probably get the CPD we want without having to put in requests, fill out forms or set cover-work. Take charge of your own CPD as much as possible.

Summary

- New teachers are often unaware of the level and nature of support available to them. This can lead to a sense of disillusion.
- Ultimately, support involves giving a teacher strategies to manage XYZ themselves in the first instance. It is only after that that higher levels of support become available.
- Save the support for when you absolutely need it. Make sure that you have tried everything in your power before making a request.
- If you are an NQT, use your mentor meetings to discuss your specific needs. Show your conscientiousness by telling your mentor what you're already doing and then ask for alternatives/improvements.
- Support for lesson planning, behaviour management, etc. may be readily available, but it is important that you do not become overly reliant on it as this can be detrimental to your professionalism.
- Just because someone is above you in the hierarchy, it doesn't mean that it's their support that you're entitled to. To get the maximum level of support, make sure you go to the right people for the right thing.
- The best CPD that you can get is by simply asking your colleagues what they do in lessons, how they teach, etc. Make a point of spending five minutes every few lunchtimes talking shop.

Chapter 12

How to be a happy teacher

If you ask most teachers whether they are happy in their jobs, you can bet your new set of glue sticks that they will give you a different answer every time you ask: literally, it will change on a weekly, daily or even hourly basis. If you are a new teacher, these emotions are more difficult to manage and you will very probably go from wanting to leave the profession in November to looking forward to seeing your classes in January. It is just a fact that the system creates a lot of emotional labour, of which this is the natural by-product.

Given the nature of our job, it is even more important for teachers to know that, like in any other situation, the way in which one responds to their circumstances is as much (if not more) of a determinant of their happiness than the circumstances themselves. With this in mind, you can learn to deal a whole lot better with the emotional rollercoaster that is teaching.

This chapter is not about wellbeing – at least, not in the conventional sense. You will not be asked to go running, take up yoga, practise mindfulness, have a hot bath or ring up a colleague and bend their ear back for 45 minutes. While all these things are indeed invaluable for wellbeing, to be a consistently happy teacher you need something greater. You need a purpose.

Clutch onto your purpose

Whether it's behaviour, data or workload, at some point (irrespective of how well managed your school is) it will get too much. That's when your mind will start to wander. That's when you need to clutch onto your purpose.

Ask yourself what made you want to be a teacher. More than likely, it's because you wanted to positively impact the life chances of young people. You wanted to be part of the making of a person. You wanted to be thanked. You wanted to be appreciated. You wanted to have fun. You wanted your words to forever be ingrained in people's minds. You wanted to be a source of stability in young people's lives. You wanted others to be as passionate about your subject as you are.

In your mind somewhere, there is likely to be a purpose, a *higher* purpose, for which you became a teacher that goes far beyond the need for an income. Identify it and clutch onto it tightly. Clutch onto it as if someone was trying to snatch it from you. Only then will you achieve the kind of happiness that you deserve.

The 'higher' your reason, the easier it will be to deal with the less desirable aspects of the education system. Every human has something, be it a principle, person or possession, for which they are willing to suffer. If you can incorporate your higher purpose for teaching into your core values, then the less bearable parts of the job will be a lot less so. On the wall of my old boxing gym, next to a large painting of a shamrock, in big green letters it read: 'How much do you wannit?' How much do you want to achieve your higher purpose?

Muhammad Ali once said, 'I hated every minute of training but I said: don't quit. Suffer now and live the rest of your life as a champion.' Decide your purpose and constantly remind yourself of it. In those cold, dark winter months when you sit in your car staring into space for ten minutes before you enter your house, remind yourself. When the pesky middle leader sends you some inane feedback on your learning walk, remind yourself. When you're told that Ofsted are coming tomorrow and they're going to observe you, remind yourself. When you read a big long thank you note from a quiet kid in your class, remind yourself. When kids cry tears of joy on results day, remind yourself. When you accidentally send the headteacher an email ending with two small 'x's, remind yourself.

And finally...

Some aspects of the education system are pesky, detrimental or somewhere in the middle. Hopefully this book has given you a range of strategies that you can employ to make the system work better for you and your pupils alike. Remember that, ultimately, education takes place in the classroom, and while it may not always feel like it, you have a lot of say over what goes on in yours.

The words and actions of a good teacher are far more powerful than any system.

Focus on the many positives. Manage the not-so-positives.

Clutch onto your purpose.

You are a champion.

Index

apathetic pupils 21–2
  being inspirational to 23
  and education system 28–9
  and grit 26–8
  lesson planning and general organisa-
    tion for 25
  problems related to 22
assessments 25, 36–7
attitude, of teachers 32–3

behaviour management 73
  consequence system 69–70
  conversations 77–8
  during Ofsted inspection 62–4
  early interventions 77–9
  phoning home 78
  priorities 76–7
  restorative approach 70–1
  rules setting 81
  seating plan 80–1
  teachers' responsibility 72
  zero-tolerance approach 70
behaviour policies 2, 63–4, 69
body language 76
book scrutinies 37–8, 59

classroom management 75–6
CPD (Continuing Professional
    Development) 103–4
current grades 44
curriculum
  accessibility 10–12
  'bin the curriculum' approach 13–14, 18, 19
  and child's skill development 11–12
  non-cognitive skills development 11–
    12, 15–19
  teaching constraints 10

data
  and Ofsted inspections 58
  problem with 43–4

emotional intelligence 95
emotional reactions 83
exam-oriented education system 28–9

improvement-oriented approach 52
intervention sessions 22, 50–1
irrelevant chats 92–4

learning walks 34, 37, 59, 61–2, 106
lesson plans/planning 33, 35, 61–2

observations 32, 61–2
  and assessment 36–7
  and attitude 32–3
  and lesson plans 33, 36
Ofsted and inspections 55–6

expectations 61
ignorance about 60–1
lesson observations and learning walks 61–2
making it fun 64–5
pupil behaviour during 62–4
and SLTs 59–60
tips for facing 65–6

peer support 103–4
performance management 39–42, 52
  evidence 40, 41–2
  pupil voice surveys 41
  targets 39–41
  TA's inputs 41
phoning home 78, 89
positive relationship building 52
  being liked by pupils 95–6
  and emotional intelligence 95
  and humour 94–5
  irrelevant chats 92–4
proactivity 63

recapping prior knowledge 12
rewards/rewarding 52
  forced rewards 86–7
  methods of 89
  rewarding high standards 88–9
  rewarding the basics 85–6, 87–8

seating plan 80–1
self-deprecating humour 94–5
self-support 102
signposts 39
SLTs, and Ofsted inspections 59–60
stress and anxiety 47–8
support
  concept of 99–100
  hierarchy 102–3
  lack of 100
  and meetings 101
  readily available support 102
  supply–demand mismatch 99
  supporting oneself 102
  time and energy requirement 101

target grades 44–5
  absorbing the pressure 46–8
  alternative message 46–7
  high levels 51–3
  and intervention 50–1
  off-grade pupils 49
  using in lessons 48–9
time management 14

underachieving pupils 49–51, 52

verbal praise 89